Other books by Claudine Burnett:

African Americans in Long Beach and Southern California: A History.

Animal Tales (Some a little fishy)

Died in Long Beach: Cemetery tales.

Fighting Fear: Long Beach in the 1940s.

From Barley Fields to Oil Town: A Tour of Huntington Beach, 1901-1922.

Haunted Long Beach.

Haunted Long Beach 2.

Murderous Intent? Long Beach, CA. 1880's-1920.

Prohibition Madness.

The Red Scare, UFOs & Elvis: Long Beach Enters the Atomic Age.

Soaring Skyward: A History of Aviation in and around Long Beach, CA.

Strange Sea Tales Along the Southern California Coast.

Jointly with other authors:

Surfing Newport Beach: The Glory Days of Corona del Mar. With Paul Burnett.

The Heritage of African Americans in Long Beach. In association with the African American Heritage Society of Long Beach, Aaron L. Day and Indira Hale Tucker.

Balboa Films: a history and filmography of the silent film studio. With Jean-Jacques Jura and Rodney Norman Bardin II.

www.claudineburnettbooks.com

The Pacific Squab and Poultry Farm

Chronicles of the Harnett Family
of Long Beach, CA

Ivy Harnett

Edited by:
Polly Harnett Johnson and Claudine Burnett

authorHOUSE®

AuthorHouse™
1663 Liberty Drive
Bloomington, IN 47403
www.authorhouse.com
Phone: 833-262-8899

Published by AuthorHouse 06/30/2023

ISBN: 979-8-8230-1100-6 (sc)
ISBN: 979-8-8230-1099-3 (e)

Library of Congress Control Number: 2023911946

Print information available on the last page.

Dedicated to the early settlers of Signal Hill and Burnett and the memories they left behind.

CONTENTS

FOREWORD
by Claudine Burnett

Polly Johnson was deeply involved in the history of Long Beach and the role her family played. In 1889 the Harnetts left England and arrived in Long Beach in October of that year. Long Beach was a small village then, with a population of just 500. In the farmland outside the city, the Harnetts started the Pacific Squab and Poultry Farm. The family of 14 children grew up in the city and as teachers, ranchers, civil servants, and businessmen contributed much to the evolution of our town.

Polly passed away in 2020, before her work on the family was completed. She was the last child, of the last child of the original family, the daughter of Frank Harnett. In 2016 we had discussed my helping her compile a book from the material she had gathered, but Polly's ill health prevented us from doing anything except talk about the project. I felt Polly would want me to finish what she and her Aunt Ivy had started so long ago. I had read some of the stories Ivy wrote and knew it had a much larger audience than just the family. It was a chronicle of the city, as well as the Harnett family.

Thanks to Polly's daughter, Martha Lenocker, who cleaned out a house full of memories, I have had access to what Polly accomplished, and I have worked on finishing the narrative. I have updated the language, corrected dates, added more historic detail, and incorporated the collection of letters and writings of other Harnett descendants into this story. It seems most of the memories shared here were talked about often in the family and the community. Sometimes their "recollections" conflicted and I have tried to trace down the facts by using newspaper, census and other records. I have also kept the names of her siblings as Ivy wrote them. It was confusing since most went by their middle name or nicknames. I've included all as an addition to the book.

I'd like to thank the Long Beach Public Library and the Historical Society of Long Beach for helping secure photos for the book, with special thanks to Jeff Whalen, Roxanne Patmore, and Jen Malone for their efforts. And great appreciation to Dr. Kaye Briegel for photo research and editing, and to Martha Lenocker for allowing me access to family records and photos.

By the way, if you are curious about my surname and the area of Long Beach known as Burnett, there is no connection.

INTRODUCTION
by Polly Harnett Johnson

Many years ago, during a Harnett family gathering which followed a funeral service for one of the Harnett sisters, I asked the cousins sitting across from me about their family — how they were, where they were living and what they were doing now. It was a lovely conversation, but soon the gathering was over and we went our separate ways. I don't remember seeing them or talking to them again, since this family did not live in southern California, nor do I remember their name or the information we shared. However, someone else did.

Years later, our family was visiting the family of another cousin, Stan Harnett, in Calabasas. We had a wonderful afternoon and as we were about to pack up and leave, Stan left the room for a few minutes. When he returned, he was carrying a box. He said something like, "Polly, now that you have expressed an interest in the family history, you should have these." He handed me the box and told me that it held the stories or "Chronicles" that Aunt Ivy (Harnett) had written about the Harnett family in Long Beach. Included were also some stories written by Josephine (Josie) Simmons another Harnett sister.

Over the years I have retrieved the box and worked on the stories, setting up a filing system and typing up some that were hand written. After my husband George and I retired, I knew this was one project I needed to take on and that it would mean serious work. The typed pages had faded. I found that many of the stories had not been completed. Some stories had notes like "insert Norah's typed story here," or "this is the same story as in section one," or "that's all of this story for now," and I really didn't know where to find the connections, so let me just have Ivy describe her project in her own words:

"There are those who might question my right as a chronicler. There are those who find the tales I told so glibly in my teens just repetitions of stories I heard others tell. My oldest sister, Bessie, with her eyes twinkling often said, 'Why Ivy, you weren't even born or thought of then.' This has been a serious handicap all the years since, but I hope you enjoy the tales of the Harnett family growing up in Long Beach, even if I borrowed some of my memories from others in the family."

I have decided to continue what Ivy started. "The Pacific Squab and Poultry Farm: Chronicles of the Harnett Family of Long Beach, CA." Are You Ready . . . Get Set . . . Go . . .

HARNETT FAMILY CHRONOLOGY

Ernest Harnett (10/7/1840-2/20/1918) – **FATHER**

Julia Sarah Berrell Harnett (11/24/1848-9/13/1928) – **MOTHER**

Jane Elizabeth Harnett (1/17/1873-2/16/1918) – **BESSIE**

Ernest Thomas Harnett (10/9/1874-7/27/1954) – **TOM**

John Abraham Harnett (7/9/1877-5/20/1944) – **JACK**

Margaret Ethel Harnett Kersting (4/14/1879-2/3/1962) – **ETHEL**

Geoffrey Berrell Harnett (5/30/1881-2/3/1884) – **GEOFFREY**

Josephine Harnett Simmons (4/9/1883-4/23/1978) – **JOSIE**

Helen Mary Harnett Morris (8/9/1884-5/27/1966) – **HELEN**

Norah Berrell Harnett Selfridge (11/8/1885-9/11/1963) – **NORAH**

Anne Hutchinson Harnett Kimball (2/16/1887-11/7/1975)
NANNY/ANNE

Edward Hutchinson Harnett (2/23/1888-1/20/1935) – **EDWARD**

Julia Caroline Harnett (4/15/1889-5/23/1907) – **CAROLINE**

Ivy Dodd Harnett (1/26/1891-3/13/1983) – **IVY**

Kathleen Harnett (12-5/1894-9/30/1991) – **KATHLEEN**

Frank Berrell Harnett (6/26/1897-12/29/1979) – **FRANK**

WHY AMERICA? WHY LONG BEACH?

Leaving England

Two wars, the Crimean War of 1853-1856, and the American Civil War (1861-1865), affected many, including my family. It is sad to say we prospered during these times of anguish and death, but we did. During these wars, gentlemen farmers in England — or the "landed gentry" as they were called — became rich.

Both wars prevented the export of grain from Russia and the United States, shielding Britain from the effects of free trade. Having 610 acres, Grandfather Thomas Harnett prospered. With lack of competition, and a series of good harvests, my grandfather bought more land, which he passed on to his sons who were starting families of their own. His daughters were not forgotten. He provided a dowry for my Aunt Julia when she married Abraham Hutchinson, and a yearly stipend for my Aunt Selina, who remained single.

My father Ernest Harnett and his brothers Alfred and Frank, were each given large farms in Kent, near the town of Newington, and 10,000 pounds each — the equivalent of $50,000 in American money — with which to maintain the farms. Alfred, the oldest was given Thrognall the old family home dating back to 1605 (though the Harnetts had only owned it since 1804). Frank was given Wormdale Farm where the family lived until Great Grandfather Thomas Harnett passed away in 1846. Then Thrognall passed to the oldest son, my grandfather, also named Thomas, which he later deeded to Alfred. Father was given the 137-acre Cambry farm on Stickfast Lane. It was located in Bobbing, a village in Kent dating back to the 14th century, only a few miles from his brothers' acreage. There, father employed five men and two boys, including Ed Gulvin, who was responsible for telling us about the wonders of Long Beach, California.

At age 49, my Father, and 41-year-old Mother decided to leave our farm during what was later called the "Great Depression of British Agriculture." This agricultural depression, which is said to have lasted from 1873 to 1896, was caused by the dramatic fall in grain prices that followed the opening up of the American prairies to cultivation in the 1870s and the advent of cheap transportation with the rise of steamships. While other countries imposed tariffs on imported grain, Britain did not. This led to even lower prices for British agricultural products. Father could no longer continue to absorb these loses and care for his family. It was time to move.

Father was a farmer who would have preferred to be a mathematician. He loved to sit by the hour and work on logarithms and problems of higher mathematics. But a farmer he became, however he did use his knowledge of mathematics in representing the parish of Newington in a number of ways. Elected to the equivalent of a city council he was often in London to discuss agricultural taxes, road repairs, and other matters regarding his area. He was known to always have detailed numbers and statistics to support his proposals. Though we never thought to ask, it seems likely he met Mother during one of his London visits. On February 8, 1872, 31-year-old Ernest married 24-year-old Julia Sarah Berrell in Lambeth church, London.

As the years rolled by, their family increased with Bessie, Tom, Jack, Ethel, Geoffrey, Josie, Helen, Norah, Edward, Anne and Caroline. But by 1889, Cambry farm was not paying and the money was dwindling.

Eleven children and the staff of servants to keep up the home and the help necessary to manage the crops — cherries and hops mostly — became a financial burden. Something had to be done. As Mother and Father talked it over it seemed more and more necessary that they move to one of three different spots in the world — Canada, America, or Australia.

Aunts and uncles from both sides of the family begged them not to leave England. They didn't want to go, but the other alternative was that two children would go to one childless aunt and uncle. Two more to still other childless relatives and so on until Mother and Father had disposed of all but five children, Bessie, Tom, Ethel, Jack and Geoffrey.

So, a decision had to be made. Would they stay in their beloved country and put out for adoption six of their remaining children? Or would they immigrate. Sadly, the choice was made easier when little Geoffrey, born in 1881, died at the age of 2 years 8 months.

I shall forever be grateful to Mother and Father for deciding to keep all my brothers and sisters together, even if it meant leaving their homeland. So that decision made, the next weighty question was — "Where to?"

The merits of British Colombia, California and Australia were considered from all angles. Mother's uncle, Edward Sullivan, was the Bishop of Algoma, Canada, and would have welcomed them to Canada. Then one day a letter arrived from California. In was from Ed Gulvin, who had been one of the horsemen at our Stickfast Lane farm. He had immigrated some years earlier and was living in Florence, a little village near Los Angeles. He wrote such glowing accounts of southern California, of the ocean, fertile soil, wonderful schools and of the equable climate. This letter was the fact that tipped the scales for California. Ed mentioned the many new towns springing up in the Southland, but one in particular appealed to Father — Long Beach — an alcohol free, religious settlement, with good rich soil, and lots of potential.

Those bidding the family goodbye felt Mother and Father were going to a country of hardship. Why leave a lovely England, with all the luxuries and comforts of the age, for a land of Indians and buffaloes? But the die was cast. The farm was sold and the ship named the *City of Chicago* was booked to bring Father and Mother and eight of their children to America. Jack and Ethel remained with Mother's uncle, Abraham Hutchinson, who was the Vicar of Eynsford. Jack was to finish his engineering course at the N.W. University and Ethel her course at the London Conservatory of Music.

It was a sad parting, made even sadder when the family was about to board the ship and a messenger brought them news of Uncle Tom's death. He was one of Mother's uncles — a physician — a surgeon like her father — a Master of the Royal College of Surgeons. They were distraught they could not stay for the funeral, but they had a ship to catch.

Atlantic Crossing

The Harnetts left England behind in October 1889. Though I would not be born until 1891, my family often spoke of their ten days on the churning Atlantic. Mother said she was wise in deciding against bringing the children's nurse, faithful though she had been, and another, a maid of ten years loyal service. "Oh, ma'am," they had pleaded. "We'll help you all the way, if you'll just take us to America with you."

Mother knew that even loyal maids and faithful nurses can be seasick and she also knew that six children under seven years of age would be quite enough to manage without looking after two seasick maids.

With no maids to help, and the two oldest children suffering sea sickness, Father helped Mother with the five youngest children — Josie, Helen, Norah, Anne, and Edward.

My parents developed a routine. Once the young Harnetts were dressed, they were put, one at a time, outside the cabin door where interested passengers, time hanging heavy on their hands, were eager to play and watch over them. My young siblings must have been entrancing, the girls in their little pinafores and long ruffled pantaloons and Edward in his Scotch kilts. After the older brood were dressed and "released," Mother bathed six-month-old Caroline. With the rolling of the ship Mother often got more of the bath water over herself than over the baby, but she bathed Caroline each morning just the same.

One morning Mother took time to take an inventory of our possessions and discovered nine very beautiful dolls given the children by their numerous English aunts and uncles missing. Deciding to ask the children about the dolls, Mother discovered Anne and Edward at

4

the ship's rail with a doll in Anne's hand. Somehow, they had escaped the observant eyes of fellow passengers who regularly watched over them. As she approached, a beautiful doll was thrown overboard to join the others now bobbing up and down in the ship's wake. A scream of delight from both children was synchronized with the splash of doll number nine.

Mother watched the bobbing dolls disappear mid Atlantic. No word was spoken. The dolls were gone — perchance the mermaids would enjoy them or so she led Josie, Norah and Helen to believe when tears brimmed in their eyes at the loss of their precious dolls. What were dolls overboard? Mother's babies had not gone over the rail with them. That was something to rejoice in.

One thing about our family is that many were not called by the names given them at birth. Jane, the oldest was christened Jane Elizabeth, but known in the family as Bessie. Tom, the eldest son, was baptized Ernest Thomas. To avoid confusion with Father we called him Tom. Both Tom and Bessie suffered severe seasickness and couldn't lift their heads from their berths the whole way across the Atlantic. Father was fine all the way. Mother said she didn't have time to be seasick, but 15-year-old Tom and 16-year-old Bessie were flattened.

Hungry, despite seasickness, Tom begged Father to bring him something to eat, but to no avail. Father had ideas about food on board ship and it was only eaten by those who were able to come to the dining room. Bessie was too ill to even ask for some morsel and her illness was made worse by the Swedish woman she shared a cabin with who devoured can after can of oily sardines in the berth above Bessie. It wasn't a helpful smell nor was the sound of the raucous voiced woman outside Bessie's door who daily reiterated, parrot like, the fatal words "You must all expect to be sick," in her twangy New York accent.

But the harrowing days aboard ship for Tom and Bessie were dimmed to insignificance when we reached New York. We landed not at Ellis Island, which wouldn't open until 1892, but Castle Garden, also known as Castle Clinton. It opened in 1855 and was run by the State of New York. No visa, or other documentation was needed for entry, only a passenger ticket.

As the ship approached Long Island, even Tom and Bessie rose from their beds to catch sight of the wonders of the city that lay ahead. Everyone was excited. There was the Statue of Liberty, dedicated three years earlier, and the rotunda of the immigration station of Castle Garden. Six miles below the city an officer from the quarantine station boarded our ship, and Mother and Father had a hard time keeping the children's enthusiasm in check.

The ship was allowed to continue to Castle Garden after the quarantine officer checked on the health of passengers. Sailing once again, we were mesmerized by the harbor, studded with crafts of every description. Then the time-consuming process of landing began.

A landing agent and customs official boarded the ship to inspect our luggage. After our luggage was checked and tagged, we were allowed to board a barge to take us to the Castle Garden pier. It was quite an ordeal. Since we were a large household there were hours upon hours of tedious red tape. There were two babes in arms. Julia Caroline, who we called Caroline, was just months old, born in the spring of 1889. Then there was twenty-month-old Edward. Father and Tom carried one baby each and one bundle from the boat to shore after all had cleared customs.

Once the family was all safely on the soil of the United States of America, we were directed down a hallway to the large rotunda. In the passage, we were met first by one government official, and then another, who scrutinized the appearance of every immigrant. We were asked questions such as names, nationality, former place of residence, and intended place of residence. After the government inspectors were satisfied, we were ushered farther into the rotunda, where we had to remain until all passengers had been questioned.

By this time, the children were hungry and crying, but food vendors would only accept American dollars. Asking where to change money, Father was directed to one of three exchange brokers in the rotunda, who exchanged foreign money for a small fee. There was a board set up listing the daily fluctuations in rates. Even with his passion for numbers, the money values confused Father, who must have been stressed dealing with immigration, baggage, and hungry children. Fortunately, Tom was able to understand the process and assure Father he wasn't being cheated. We had heard much about unscrupulous individuals who took advantage of the new arrivals, but learned that the money changers inside the rotunda had been checked for their honesty.

Father then set off to purchase rail tickets to California. He was directed to agents of the railroad companies, who sold passage to all parts of the United States and Canada. These agents had also been checked for their honesty, and Father was happy to learn he wouldn't be at risk of fraud or extortion, which often happened outside the immigration station.

Tickets in hand, and bellies full, we boarded a ferry, which took us to the train station. There was one awful moment when Father went on some errand and the ferry began to pull away from the dock. Father was nowhere to be seen. While we waited on the ferry, some of the children began weeping vociferously and Mother, Bessie and Tom, searched the ferry frantically for Father. As the space of water widened the screams grew louder, Father appeared, and together we marveled at the city before us. Finally reaching the city proper, Mother tried to calm four-year-old Norah, who was terrified by the New York traffic. It marked Norah for life, even today the traffic of a large city always terrifies her.

A Train Ride to Long Beach

We were heading west to southern California, which had only been assessable by rail since 1876. Though northern California opened with the arrival of the Southern Pacific in 1869, it meant little to those in southern California, separated from the rail terminus by 450 miles of dirt roads or open seas. But the railroad finally reached the southern portion of the state on September 5, 1876, and brought

Long Beach city founder William Willmore to the area. Willmore founded the American Colony, where we were headed.

We made our way to southern California at a time of intense railroad competition. Another railroad, the Atchison Topeka and Santa Fe arrived in the area in 1887 and a price war developed between the two competing rail lines. Rail travel dropped from $100 ($3,235 in 2021) to $1 ($27) in March 1887, which would have encouraged a man with such a large family to head to southern California.

My parents and their eight children travelled via several railroads until they reached New Orleans which had a direct Southern Pacific connection to Los Angeles. After four days of train travel, they reached their destination in November 1889. Ed Gulvin was there to greet them and my family stayed in Florence for two months with Ed Gulvin's family. Mr. Gulvin, if you remember, had been one of the horsemen at our Stickfast Lane farm in Kent.

From the accounts Father had read, and glowing narratives from Ed, we had decided to settle near the new town of Long Beach, established in 1882. Unfortunately, soon after our arrival heavy rains flooded the area and railroad service to our new home was interrupted, which forced us to stay with the Gulvins longer than we had anticipated.

That winter of 1889-1890 was one of the worst in city history. Keeping the passenger trains operating was a top priority. Washouts were frequent between Dominguez and Watson Station, the only line into Long Beach. When through lines were impossible, trains at either end of the line from Los Angeles to Long Beach would shuttle back and forth with passengers forced to cross the washout on temporary trestles. Around Christmas train service stopped all together. The flooding made Long Beach a virtual island. The flat area between Long Beach and Wilmington was under six feet of water. The water rushing in the rivers was so swift that the 2600-acre Nadeau vineyard, east of where we were staying in Florence, was devastated. People were stranded in Los Angeles for a week, unable to get home. One man made it back to Long Beach by swimming three stretches of flood water!

On January 1, 1890, during a brief interlude when the rail line opened, our family arrived in Long Beach. Rains began again the following week. Long Beach was shut off from all outside communication for three more weeks until the flood waters receded. Freight service, which transported all our possessions, was impossible for nearly two months. What a welcome! In telling me this story, Tom said 34 inches of rain fell that season.

At that time, the only rail line to Long Beach was the Southern Pacific. The Harnett household was met at the depot by Reverend Sidney Kendall of the Congregational Church who escorted our sizable family to his home at Third and Cedar, where we remained a few days. Then we moved to a ten-acre farm at Tenth and Elm which we rented from a Dr. Williams. Years later St. Mary's Hospital was built on the land. I remember my brother Tom, who was a patient there, tell the nuns that he had raised corn under his bed! They thought he was crazy and mentioned their concern to my brother Frank who laughingly explained Tom wasn't crazy, the family had once tilled the land!

Later the nuns asked more about early Long Beach and Tom remarked that it was a lonesome drive through the fields in those days to get to downtown Long Beach. There were just a couple of little wheel ruts in the center of American Avenue (now Long Beach Blvd.) and wild plants grew so tall they hid my sister Anne. When they called her for dinner one evening, she didn't come and they feared the worst. Apparently, Anne had fallen asleep in the tall weeds and eventually woke up to hear the call. She dutifully headed home, the wheel ruts guiding her.

The ranch at Tenth and Elm was valued by Dr. Williams at $2,400 ($74,000 in 2021), and our yearly rent was one-tenth of that amount. We thought the figure pretty high and soon saved money to buy five acres from Mr. Saunders, out of town, on Atlantic near Twenty-fifth Street (2481 Atlantic), where Father also rented near-by acreage on the north side of Signal Hill. Here, on what came to be called the Pacific Squab and Poultry Farm, the family raised fruit and vegetables, along with 2,000 chickens, 10 cows, and 12 pigs. There were also 5,000 pigeons, whose young were called squab.

The Southern Pacific was the only rail line to Long Beach before the arrival of the Terminal Railroad in 1891 and the Pacific Electric in 1902. Farmers in the Signal Hill area were anxious to have their own rail station to get their produce to market sooner. Ranchers in the area contacted Thomas Burnett, general manager of the Terminal Railroad and he agreed to build a station on the northwest corner of California and Burnett Street, the street named in honor of such an accommodating gentleman. It was originally called the Signal Hill station but it seemed the post office didn't like compound or hyphenated names for their post office stations and the name was changed to Burnett in February 1897. What about the name "Long Beach?" It wasn't until 1911, after numerous petitions, that the post office agreed to change Longbeach to Long Beach! In 1901 the Terminal Railroad became the Salt Lake and Terminal Railroad when the line was extended to Salt Lake City. By that time the whole area around our farm was known as Burnett, which continued to be our postal address for years to come.

Settling in Burnett

Burnett, which would be annexed to Long Beach in 1910, was the first station out of Long Beach to the north on the Salt Lake railroad line. Burnett's fertile soil and climate meant that flowers and fruits could be raised year-round. It was not unusual for the railroad to pick up 400 pounds of flowers and berries each day to take to market. A large cannery operated on the forty-acre Densmore Ranch in Burnett. There 4000-gallon cans of blackberries and 600 cans of jams and preserves of figs and other kinds of fruit were put up during the summer.

As the train rounded the corner onto Willow Street and California Avenue, the bridge over the rail tracks came into view. There was a deep cut. Just after the cut there was along trestle with a hollow below. Daring youngsters, including my sister Helen, sometimes walked this trestle, ignoring the danger that a train might suddenly appear. One neighbor boy claimed he liked to cling to the underside of the outer rails of the trestle when trains roared past. We weren't sure to believe him since we had never seen him do so, and we knew boys have a tendency to brag, especially in front of girls!

However, we were fearless and not to be outdone by boys. Helen was very much an acrobat and didn't get dizzy in high places. Mother would have had a nervous breakdown had she known of our escapades on that bridge. Helen used to walk across the top rail and the slightest misstep would have toppled her into the cut some thirty feet below. Caroline wasn't quite as nimble, but she was fearless and once slipped as she tried to match the prowess of her older sister. Grabbing the railing, a four-inch splinter was driven under the main tendons on her wrist and she had to be taken to a doctor. Needless to say, she received a stern lecture.

The northbound train would sometimes stop at the Burnett Station which was south of the bridge. Then it would again proceed uphill. As children, we tried to be there when the train headed up hill. Much to our glee, we would be treated to the sound of the train whistle and a billowing, suffocating cloud of smoke. The train followed California Avenue north. It rose out of the cut, up the grade, and made a broad curve to the east toward Cherry Avenue. Then it was out of sight. On the return trip down the hill the train would once again appear, this time coming around the bend and heading south. I think the engineers were always careful when whey entered the deep cut with the Willow Street bridge over it. It was hard not to spot the youngsters playing "I dare you!" Fortunately, the train never ran over any of the young daredevils.

The whistle of the train told us what to expect. When a stop at the Burnett Street Station was planned, it issued a long whistle and two short toots. When there was only one long whistle, we children cowered in fascination while the train roared past, its metal arm reaching out of the mail car to seize the mail bag, which was on a tall pole. Then the incoming mail bag was flung from the mail car door with considerable force to make sure the rush of air did not send it under the wheels. I remember once the force was not enough and the bag ripped. I well recall that instance because the bag contained a book I had long been waiting for, sent to me from England, which ended up mutilated.

Sometimes the trains went by at night and I still remember how I enjoyed listening to the long toot and waiting to hear whether or not the train would stop at the station. Then I would dream of the many places I might travel on a train. Of course, that particular train would not go far. From Burnett Station it went straight south to Ocean Avenue where it turned and went no farther than Terminal Island. But my imagination had no limits.

We didn't need to go to downtown Long Beach to get all our supplies. Warner Kellum had a small store on the west side of California Avenue, opposite Burnett Street. From here he ran the post office and was also an agent for the Wells Fargo Express. The mail train whistle was the signal for neighbors to gather, usually in front of his store. We children all rushed to try to be on time to see the train come in, and then we waited for the mail to be sorted.

Children were the most frequent mail collectors unless a grownup had arrived on the train, then adults would gather to learn what was happening elsewhere. Judge Dillon, who had a home on the top of Signal Hill, used the Burnett Station to take him to and from Los Angeles and he loved to pass the time of day with neighbors telling them of the latest goings on in Los Angeles.

199 S. S. City of Chicago

The ship that brought the Harnetts to America.
Source: C. Burnett

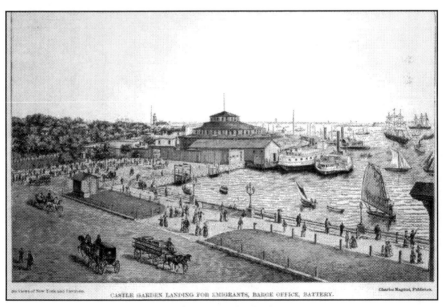

CASTLE GARDEN LANDING FOR EMIGRANTS, BARGE OFFICE, BATTERY.

Landing at Castle Garden.
Courtesy of Wikipedia

Burnett Station c. 1900.
Source: C. Burnett

View from Signal Hill c. 1890.
Courtesy of the Long Beach Collection, Long Beach Public Library

SCHOOL

Burnett School

Our school house stood at the corner of Hill Street and Atlantic Avenue. Lafayette Saunders donated one block of his 80-acre farm so his four children would not have to go all the way to the Pine Avenue School at 6th and Pine. The Burnett school room was 20 x 40-feet, and opened in September 1888.

A few years later, Mr. Saunders, Father, and others in the neighborhood planted eucalyptus trees around the school house area, partly for shade and partly as hitching posts for those who came to school on horseback. On the day the tree planting began Father asked that the American flag be flown from the school house belfry. He had just become a naturalized citizen in the new land and wanted to celebrate, showing all his patriotic heart.

Following the flag raising, the men began to plant trees in one large area to hide the otherwise conspicuous outhouses. Later many of these trees still stood on the grounds and along Lime Avenue where lawns and shrubs covered the area where the two large outhouses once stood. I remember there was a high white fence that separated these privies from the Saunders' sheep and goats at the rear of the school house, and that open grain fields surrounded the whole area except for the Saunders' home, barns and fruit trees a block to the north.

It was a one room school house that included an ante room for our coats and sweaters. All grades to the ninth attended. The small seats were in front. A large wood stove stood in the corner near the teacher's desk which was on a small platform. The platform became a stage on Friday afternoons when we stood on it to give our weekly recitations. A water bucket stood in one corner, in case the stove caught fire. There was no pencil sharpener, instead the teacher and some of the pupils carried sharp knives to sharpen the lead pencils, but chalk slates were most commonly used.

The front yard of the school house had a water faucet. There was room enough in the yard for a few horses that had been ridden to class and for the dogs who followed their masters to school. There was room outside for play — tag, jump rope, jacks, kick the can, marbles, blind man's bluff and of course various ball games. But the most fun was when the big boys would get a rope off a horse and try to lasso the little ones. Sometimes our activities got a bit out of hand. Bessie, who taught at Burnett for a while, once received a note from a parent beseeching her to put a stop to some pupils who were pulling hairs from the horses' tails to make hair rings and brooches!

There were days when the Santana wind blew. Coming through the Santa Ana canyon with little to impede its force, the clouds of dust swirled about Long Beach with such force and density that our sister Caroline got sand pneumonia. Though she coughed a lot, and had shortness of breath, she recovered in a few days.

Everyone played outside, dust storm or no dust storm. The wind brought enormous tumbleweeds which whirled across the grain fields. Younger school children like myself liked to run across Hill Street into an open field and drag out a tumbleweed and set it in the road. The wind would pick it up, and we raced after it until it got too far ahead of us and we would go back for another one.

The big boys had their excitement when a coyote chanced by looking for a meal of ground squirrel or burrowing owl. The coyotes stirred the dogs into a frenzy, much to the glee of the male population. Perhaps most fun was walking around a ground owl to see if it really would twist its head off by following your walk with its gaze. Much to out disappointment, no owl ever lost its head. In a blink of an eye, it would suddenly jerk its head back in place, so quickly none of us could see it!

Visitors to the school were quite an event. Of course, the superintendent of the county came at least once a year as did the trustees. But what an exciting thing it was to have one's mother or father visit. These were special occasions, and many of these visits coincided with our Friday closing exercises in which we proudly recited poems we had memorized.

Josie remembered one Friday when she had selected as her recitation Tennyson's *Death of the Flowers*, and claimed she put into it all the pathos she could manage, but the boys in the room laughed, which made Josie cry. The next time she chose the *Charge of the Light Brigade,* which definitely caught their attention and cheers.

My sister Anne was the star performer. Nannie, we called her then, was little and chubby and loved to recite, especially the poems of James Whitcomb Riley. She always won applause. The next family member, Edward, was different. He had a very retiring disposition and had a hard time facing an audience. When Edward was in the second grade he had a piece to speak, but bashfulness overcame him and he could not utter a word. Our teacher, Mr. Tucker, tried to prod him along for Mr. Tucker was anxious to catch the Salt Lake train to Los Angeles. When someone told Mr. Tucker the train was coming, he quickly dismissed the class and ran over the open fields, his long legs flying and his coat tails flapping. Edward was saved, for a time.

If it was a rainy day, we would often go to school barefooted. Our family believed the saying: "If the child gets his shoes wet on the way to school his feet will stay damp and cold most of the day. If he runs barefoot through the puddles his feet are dry as soon as they get into the warm school." Here in southern California that proved a sensible suggestion, and was commonly observed.

Walking home was fun with or without shoes, even though the streets were dusty and full of chuckholes. There was a mulberry tree in the Saunders' front yard. It bore quite heavily and there were days when Mrs. Saunders spread a big canvas sheet under the tree and allowed us to shake the tree so we might feast on the juicy fruit which stained our lips and fingers. Once home we would find Mother, sitting in the window with a basket of stockings on her lap to be darned. A never-ending chore.

My sister Bessie received a teacher's certificate from the State of California by passing a comprehensive test. Her education in England had taught her many things and she was able to forgo attending classes at the teacher's college in Los Angeles. Soon she was teaching eight grades in the one-room Burnett school house until she and two other teachers were asked to transfer to the new Long Beach High School in 1895.

Being a teacher didn't just involve teaching, it entailed other duties and "proper" conduct. Rules were established across the United States in the years following the Civil War up to the years leading to World War I when restrictions began to "soften." They included:

- Teachers must not drink alcohol or smoke cigarettes, be seen in any saloon, pool parlor, or smoking room, for teachers must maintain a pure moral character.
- Female teachers must not be seen in the company of a man in any buggy or carriage (or later, automobile) unless he is a brother or father.
- Teachers may not marry during the term of their contract.
- Teachers must be at home between 8:00 pm and 6:00 am.
- Female teachers may not dye or color their hair or cut it short. They must not wear lip rouge and their dresses must cover their ankles.
- Teachers must clean lamp chimneys and fill lamps, bring in a bucket of water and wood for the stove, clean outhouses, sweep floors daily and scrub weekly.
- Teachers must arrive one hour early to start a fire so the school room is warm by 9:00 am.

This was the life required of being a teacher, but it was a profession Bessie loved. When she was asked to teach at the new high school she was elated. She was replaced at the Burnett school by Nettie Frazier, a beautiful blond-haired woman with blue eyes and a very lovely pink and white complexion.

Most of the students were obedient, except for Julian Wardlow who refused to do what he was told. Back then students were punished if they did not obey. Sitting in a corner was one punishment, another was having one's knuckles slapped by a yardstick. Julian sat just in front of me and once when his conduct become disruptive, he refused to quiet down. Miss Frazier started down the aisle with a heavy yard stick and Julian hopped out of his seat and stood belligerently with an open knife in his hand shouting, "I'll show you blood! I'll show you blood!"

Undeterred, Miss Frazier, ruler gripped firmly, came on down the aisle. Julian flourished his knife but that didn't stop her. If you have ever heard the sound of an oak wood yardstick slapped flat upon the top of an oak desk you will know something of the loud bang our teacher brought forth as she said, "Sit down and give me that knife!" It worked. Just why I cannot say. Julian sat down and gave her the knife. She returned to her desk but studying was over for us all. We scarcely breathed. Our nerves were shattered and it took the morning recess and the noon lunch hour for all of us to settle back into some sort of normalcy.

Julian had an older brother, David Wardlow, and one day Mark Strode and David began a squabble that lasted several days. The angry words escalated until David's anger got the better of him. He went to Mr. Saunders' barn and "borrowed" an axe. I don't know who else was there but I remember standing on the north side of the school house watching David sharpen the weapon. Nettie Frazier stood beside him, white as a sheet, begging and pleading him to take the axe back. "No," he said over and over again, despite her attempts to calm the situation. Finally, she did what many women have done before and since. She cried. David was unprepared for this outburst and quickly relinquished the axe. After a while lessons resumed and somehow the day, and the feud among the boys, came to an end, David returning the axe to the Saunders' farm.

The Wardlows were an interesting family. In 1903, 16-year-old Mary disobeyed her parent and went off in a wagon with four young boys. Mary had been told by her parents it was not proper for her to accept a ride in a carriage with the boys and in doing so could ruin her reputation. Mary yelled at her parents and was sent to her room for her disrespect and tantrum. Still incensed at her parent's refusal to let her go out for some innocent fun, Mary escaped through her window and went in search of her male companions. When her father discovered Mary was gone, he gathered his 18-year-old son, David, and his gun and set off after her.

David was more agile than his father and it was David who first came across the buggy containing his sister, A.J. Daley, James Hill, John Stevens and Clarence Fetterman. David shouted at them to stop and when they refused, he fired his rifle loaded with bird shot at the group. The sound of the gun excited the horses and they sped into town with David in hot pursuit. Upon reaching Long Beach, Daley went to the police station and swore out a warrant against young Wardlow for assault with intent to commit murder. David was arrested, apparently having no idea of the severity of the charge, and taken to county jail.

During the trial the men told of meeting Mary on the road and asking her to go riding. She agreed and later joined them. The four young men said they were completely surprised when David fired at them. David testified he hadn't meant to kill anyone; he just hoped to stop the buggy and get his sister back. A sympathetic judge waived a prison term but fined David $30 ($900 in 2021) for his marksmanship. David and Mary's story made the local newspaper. After that we weren't allowed to associate with the family, except at school. Despite the family's somewhat tarnished reputation, they did have a street named after them!

I don't want you to get the idea that my school days were one horrible fright after another. We had wonderful times, too. On Washington's birthday there was a picnic on Signal Hill, unless it rained. Family members used to laugh when they recalled how a few months after they settled on that ten-acre ranch on Tenth and Elm, Josie, Helen and Norah walked hand in hand from home to the Pine Avenue School, at Sixth and Pine, the largest school in the district and one able to afford a custodian. These three little English girls found the school house doors closed and no one except the janitor. He told them it was Washington's birthday so there was to be no school. That was a surprise. This new country had some strange customs, along with holidays, to get used to.

By the time we younger Harnetts were in school, we did know all about Washington's birthday. It was a day we all anticipated. Burnett school children gathered at the school house and walked to Signal Hill. Each carried their own lunch and Nettie Frazier always had some surprise — usually candy — for all of us. There might have been 30 of us and it was a real tragedy if measles or chicken pox kept some away.

Boys! I remember one ate his pie first — three pieces — because he was afraid sandwiches and boiled eggs might take the edge off his appetite and he wouldn't be able to eat enough pie. Another boy entertained us all by crawling in as far as he could into a badger hole.

When we had eaten to bursting, we rolled down the grassy slopes of Signal Hill and wandered at will in and out of its canyons. There was one canyon some of us never dared enter. It was on the east slope and quite deep with treacherous cliffs.

I suppose the older boys enjoyed having it to themselves after they had filled us younger ones with wild tales of a headless horseman who went charging through brandishing a flaming sword. They claimed a man had been killed as he rode his horse through the canyon and his and the horse's skeletons were supposed to be there. Their stories worked. We never went near enough even to peek over the steep sides. I don't know how Miss Frazier ever collected everyone for the return home, but I don't seem to remember anyone ever being lost in the deep recesses of the canyons for the coyotes or the headless horseman to find.

I was eleven when the Pacific Electric railroad began to transform Long Beach. When the first line was built in 1902, workers uprooted the eucalyptus trees that had been growing down the middle of American Avenue as far as Anaheim Road. The line was too far away for my sisters Josie and Norah who started Normal School, a four-year teacher's college in Los Angeles, in 1900. Instead, they took the nearby Salt Lake train to classes until 1904 when the electric line expanded with a line to Huntington and Newport Beach, with the right-of-way cut through the northeast corner of our ranch.

My sisters found the Pacific Electric, also called the "Red Car," had more frequent runs and decided to use it. They boarded at Willowville, just North of Willow Street on Long Beach Boulevard. From there passengers could ride north into Los Angeles, south into downtown Long Beach or south-west towards Newport Beach, Balboa and Huntington Beach. They enjoyed the trip, especially in the spring when great fields of mustard, golden poppies and wild roses grew along the way. Some mornings they left home early, walking a few feet into the willow thicket near the Red Car line and picked an armful of flowers to take with them.

With the electric line to Long Beach expanding, some things did not change fast enough to meet the needs of the new inhabitants who settled along the new transportation route. Such was the case with the Burnett school. In 1902, a number of families moved to the area from Oklahoma and two new rooms had to be added to the schoolhouse. Before the addition the school had 72 pupils in a room for 48.

Josie and Norah both completed their work at the Los Angeles teacher's college at 5th and Grand in June of 1904. When the Normal School opened in 1882 it had a 3-year-course of study which allowed graduates to teach grammar school. In 1893, it expanded classes to a 4-year-program certifying graduates to teach to 9th grade. In 1919 the school became the foundation for the University of California, Los Angeles.

Today we may look back on past education standards as basic or rudimentary, even primitive, so I thought I would include a list of questions students had to answer in order to graduate from 8th grade. They included spelling, reading, arithmetic, grammar, geography, physiology, civil government and history. Here are a few (more at the end of the book)

- At $1.62 a cord, what would be the cost of a pile of wood 24 ft. long, 4 ft. wide and 6 ft. 3 inches high?
- Adjectives have how many Degrees of Comparison?
- Name and give the capitals of States touching the Ohio River.
- How does the liver compare in size with other glands?
- Define the following forms of government: Democracy, Limited Monarchy, Absolute Monarchy, Republic. Give examples of each.
- Name the last battle of the Civil War; War of 1812; French and Indian War, and the commanders of each battle.

Yes, a lot to instill in the minds of students, especially when teachers were teaching several grades at once, AND the questions weren't known before the test! That was the life my sisters chose.

I remember Josie and Norah's Normal School graduation ceremony. The auditorium was packed to capacity, with around 60 graduates, all dressed in white. Following graduation Josie became one of 16 teachers at the Atlantic Avenue school. Norah's assignment found her at Burnett, she and Jesse White were the only teachers, with Mr. Huff as Principal. My sister Kathleen and brother Frank were students there, with Norah as their teacher. Frank, later in life used to laugh saying that until he graduated high school he never had a class that didn't have a sister in the classroom or a sister teaching it!

The Burnett area continued to grow, and the 1903 addition to the school was soon too small. The Burnett school was in desperate need of an upgrade.

By 1908 there were 177 students, taught by 4 teachers, including Norah, in a building that consisted of three rooms and a shed. On windy days the walls moved and the windows were often blown from their casements. Besides the 177 students there were another 88 children who couldn't attend the school because there wasn't enough room for them. They were forced to travel a distance to the Alamitos Heights, Pine Avenue and Daisy Avenue schools. A bond election passed and soon there was a three story, brick school, with a shingle roof. There were 9 classrooms and a large assembly room. Best of all there were indoor toilets as well as space for a cooking class — the outhouses Father helped hide were no longer needed.

Norah, Anne and I decided the assembly room needed a theater group and established the Burnett Amateur Dramatic Club. In January 1909, we put on the play "Miss Oakley's Telephone." Of course, all three of us were in it, along with Frank, Edward, Josie and Martha Spur. We raised $30 ($932 in 2021), which went towards buying equipment for the school.

Also in 1909, Clarence Coseboom, who lived on Signal Hill, offered to donate land for another school. Many believed he was doing so to help clear the family name. It had been tarnished when his 18-year-old son Walter was sent to prison in December 1903 for stealing confiscated liquor from Long Beach city hall. It was certainly a blow to Mr. Coseboom, a teetotaler, that his son took to alcohol, and was brazen enough to try to steal confiscated booze from city hall, along with friends J.S. Saunders and Carl Jordan. To make matters worse, Carl Jordan was shot trying to escape. Carl later died of blood poisoning while still hospitalized.

Mr. Coseboom was not free of sin himself. In 1896 he was elected as a City Trustee, giving his word he wouldn't interfere with the operation of McCarthy's saloon as long as the business was conducted in an orderly fashion. As soon as he was elected, however, he voted to close the saloon. The next day someone hanged an effigy in Pacific Park (now Lincoln Park). The straw stuffed figure had no name, but it had only one leg. Everyone knew it could only be Coseboom who, too, only had one leg.

The city was now without a saloon tax, which was the major source of funding for the town of 550. This led to the disincorporation of the city in 1896 and a fight to keep Long Beach alcohol free. Father was one of the anti-saloon advocates who rallied to resurrect the city and re-incorporate. He and others were upset that taxes had been raised by the county, but the tax money hadn't trickled down. The lights on the pier were shut off, streets remained unsprinkled, and weeds permeated public places. There was no money to pay for maintenance. Mr. Coseboom and others from the Law and Order League pushed for an election in April 1898, which led to Long Beach once again being an incorporated city.

Portions of the old Burnett school building were put to good use. The middle section (20 x 50 feet), was transported to a 100 x 150-foot corner lot on the north slope of Signal Hill to house the Coseboom school. Another 22 x 38-foot section was moved to the Alamitos Heights school at Temple and 17th Street to serve as a home economics classroom. The third section was given as partial payment to the moving company, Bucey & Huckstep, along with $300 ($9220 in 2021). They thought they could convert and sell the third section as a residence.

In the 1920s and 1930s, the school district decided to change the names of their schools to reflect important people in history, however Burnett residents would have none of that. Their school was known as Burnett and Burnett it would stay. The school district did not think Thomas Burnett was important enough to have a school named after him.

He had only been involved with the Salt Lake railway for six years when in 1896 he suffered a stroke and remained bedridden until his death in 1901. If he had lived his name may have been as well-known as Henry Huntington. It was his ambition to see his railway become a link in a transcontinental system, which it did when it was absorbed by the Union Pacific. He was a mover and shaker who died at the too young age of 57. In 1933, the Long Beach School District in looking for a famous Burnett to keep the name of the school the same, found Peter Burnett, California's first governor. Thomas Burnett's short history with the railroad and Long Beach was forgotten.

In 1910, the area known as Burnett was absorbed into Long Beach, only the name Burnett Street remained to mark the location. In September 2014, the Burnett school was renamed the Bobbie Smith Elementary School after charges that Peter Burnett was an alleged racist. The real history of the name was forgotten.

The High School

The Tabernacle, established in 1885 was the city's first auditorium. It stood on Third and Locust until 1905. A chapel attached to it served as our first high school. The first classes began September 16, 1895. Professor W. S. Bailey, former principal of the Pine Avenue school was appointed teacher. The school opened with 34 students, but by November, as members of our family and others from the Burnett area joined, the enrollment had increased to 44.

As I remember, the building was broad and low, fairly large, surrounded by eucalyptus trees. I attended Methodist Sunday school classes there, before there was any Episcopal church in Long Beach. In the summer, Chautauqua and camp meetings were held on the site, with people living in tents on the spacious grounds, which covered an entire block.

Then came 1897 when bonds were voted to build a permanent high school. Many people seemed to think the Tabernacle should have been the location of the high school, feeling Eighth and American was too far out of town. But that was not to be, the four-acre site at Eighth and American was purchased from the Graves family for $1500 ($50,600 in 2021) and a formal high school building erected. The following year (1898) the high school opened. Teachers included: Howard Lunt, principal and teacher of English and civics; Elmer Hall, vice-principal and teacher of science and mathematics; our sister Bessie, Latin and History; Louis Callow, Latin, Greek and German.

Getting there was a bit difficult for our family. We had to travel up and down hills all the way, for American Avenue (later Long Beach Boulevard) had not yet been leveled.

Bessie was teaching at Long Beach High School when a rally turned disruptive. The April 4, 1908, occurrence was all students and faculty talked about for weeks to come. Around midnight about 300 students from the high school marched down American Avenue, and began singing and shouting and firing blank gun cartridges into the air. Officer Gallemore, on duty that night, hearing the shooting and thinking some disaster had occurred, hurried to the scene. He arrived at Seventh and American (Long Beach Boulevard) in time to see one of the Huffmans (I think it was Henry), fire a revolver into the night. Officer Gallemore placed him under arrest and headed for the police station when Gallemore was stopped by a crowd of students, who protested the arrest, calling the policeman all sorts of vile names. Finally, one in the crowd suggested they go and tear down the jail. A worried Gallemore notified the rest of the police force to prepare for a mob; concerned citizens also joined the police to meet the rebellious teens.

The mob of students, both boys and girls, gathered in front of the jail demanding Huffman's release yelling that unless he was freed they would storm the jail. Others shouted they would beat up any police officer they saw the first chance they got. Chief of Police Williams, aroused from his bed, rushed to the scene. He remained calm, kept his temper and told students he would not release Huffman, and unless the crowd dispersed, he would put them all in jail.

The arrival of several parents, however, soon brought things to a close. The crowd began to melt away and the threatened demolition of the jail was averted. Huffman was later released and when he appeared before the judge the following morning, meek and subdued, he admitted his foolish actions. After a lecture on violation of the law he was released.

What brought about such action on the part of the students, you ask? They were celebrating the debating club's victory over Monrovia that evening.

It wasn't the high school boys, but Long Beach girls that won the city's first state basketball honors. Bessie was a teacher and Kathleen a student at the time. The team's speed and talent was so great, they trounced the Santa Monica girls' team 62 to 1 on January 29, 1910. This was followed by securing the county championship on February 12th by a 38 to 7 win over the U.S.C. Academy. On February 19th they defeated Ontario, the Orange Belt League champs, 40 to 19, and on February 26th, clinched the southern California pennant by defeating

Orange, 42 to 7. The state championship game against Lowell on May 28, 1910, followed.

The game was played on the Long Beach High School grounds and was witnessed by the largest crowd that ever attended a basketball contest in this city up to that time.

We could not but think of Caroline and her love of basketball, and how she was on the high school squad in 1905. Her team "The High School Midgets" was asked to christen the basketball court at the YMCA in May 1905. Her impressive skill as forward, led to a 19-2 victory over their competition "The Brownies."

I think Kathleen wished she was on the school's 1910 team, but tennis was her sport of choice. In any case, I was there with many of my siblings, including 13-year-old Frank who was trying not to be too impressed with the female players and their accomplishments.

It looked like Long Beach was the underdog because an extra player had to be added to the team just days before the much-heralded event. The rules both teams followed were different. In northern California the team consisted of seven players, in southern California there were only six. In state championship games northern California rules were followed. Kathleen's classmate Maizie Kendall was added as an extra jumping center to the Long Beach team. The Long Beach girls had only three days to get used to this added player and incorporate her into their game plan. Hours of extra practice paid off. The championship game was played in three periods, each ten minutes in length with 15-minute rest periods between. The Long Beach team was in the lead all the way, the score being 11 to 3 at the end of the first period and 15 to 5 at the end of the second. Bessie's students Verna Tinklepaugh and Jessie Stone were forwards on the Long Beach team; Esther Dayman, Maizie Kendall and Elsie Robinson were centers; Myra Taylor and Helen Perkins guards.

The San Franciscans had lost one of their best players due to an injury sustained in practice, but the locals were also deprived of the services of Elsie Weber who hurt herself in a practice session. The final score was 16 to 9. The contest brought to Long Beach its first State championship in any athletic sport.

The Long Beach team was so good that the following year Verna Tinklepaugh, manager of the team, received money to have a pennant made proclaiming the Long Beach team as champions of southern California for the fifth year. The ironic thing was that Long Beach won the championship without playing a single game. All the other teams had withdrawn from the Southern California Women's Basketball League; they had been beaten so badly by Long Beach in the past they didn't see any point in playing the team again.

The women's basketball achievements were the last hurrah for the high school before the new Poly High School building replaced it. Over the years several rooms and an upper story had been added to the old Long Beach High School. But the heating plant, built only for a small building, became inadequate, and had to be over fueled to keep the building warm on cold winter days. Fortunately, the principal, Mr. McCutchan, knew this and had plenty of fire drills.

The fire gong hung in the lower front hall and the office was upstairs. Once, two women coming to visit the school while all classroom doors were closed, not knowing where to go, gave a timid pull on the rope of the bell, hoping to attract someone's attention. The deluge of students pouring out of every door and down the stairway proved almost too much for the visitors. However, when a fire erupted in the building one winter morning, every student was safely evacuated. Plenty of good preparation had paid off.

It was not many years later that the old high school building became too small and too far downtown, for the growing town. A new high school, Long Beach Polytechnic opened at 16th and Atlantic in 1911.

Bessie was happy to have a new high school building to teach in. Frank, Kathleen and I were anxious to attend. Kathleen graduated in 1912. Both Frank and I in 1915 right before the Long Beach Board of Education decided that many girls and boys in high school paid more attention to each other than to their studies. At age 24, I was older than most graduates. A buggy accident when I was four, meant years of surgery on my eyes which kept me from regularly attending school.

The Board started a campaign to segregate the sexes in September 1916, asking for a $150,000 ($3.82 million in 2021) bond to build an all-girls' high school. Though the Board claimed they weren't planning this segregation for moral reasons, others knew differently. For months there had been talk of "immoral" activities at the high school with students more interested in partying, pranks, and each other than school work.

One of Bessie's students was Foster Strong. He was also a friend of Frank's. Foster's mother was on the school board and when school officials found out about a high school booze party held on campus in January 1916, students were sure Foster had snitched. Young Foster was stripped naked by fellow students and thrown into the cold waters of a pond on Willow Street. Though Foster recognized all his captors, he refused to name names. An arrest, four suspensions from the high school and a probe into an alleged liquor party held on the campus resulted.

Mischief continued. In April 1916, Bessie and other teachers at Poly High were surprised to find every keyhole in the school filled with plaster and the janitor locked and tied in his closet. Students were blamed. The teachers were able to get the classroom doors open in time to admit the pupils, causing no delays in the classroom schedules. Things had certainly gotten out of hand, and something had to be done.

Dances were forbidden in the high school as were silk socks and loud ties by boys and powder puffs, rouge and low-necked blouses for girls. High school fraternities were banned, because of their defiance of school policies. In order to enroll at Poly High School in the fall of 1916 students were asked to prove that they were not affiliated with any fraternity and if their proof was not sufficient, they were refused admission.

America's entry into World War I put a temporary halt to the campaign for a separate high school for girls, while the male graduates of 1916 went off to war.

I remember Bessie talking about Poly High School coach, Edgar Kienholtz. She and others at the school were startled when his name was listed as "failing to respond" for military' examination. Mr. Kienholtz had left Long Beach shortly after June 5, 1917, for his father's ranch in Alberta, Canada, and when he was re-elected Poly coach for the coming year no word was heard from him. His draft resistance was turned over to the federal authorities. Mr. Kienholtz later returned to Long Beach and despite the appeals of Superintendent W.L. Stephens and Principal David Burcham, who felt that finding another with Mr. Kienholz's skills would be next to impossible, Mr. Kienholz was drafted. He returned after the war to resume his old job.

Burnett school c.1900.
Courtesy Historical Society of Long Beach

The Tabernacle: Long Beach's first high school.
Courtesy of the Long Beach History Collection, Long Beach Public Library

Long Beach High School c.1895.
Courtesy Wikipedia

Early Poly High School c. 1911.
Courtesy Historical Society of Long Beach

Pine Avenue School, 1902.
Courtesy of the Long Beach History Collection, Long Beach Public Library

HORSE AND BUGGY DAYS

Willmore City

We like to say we grew up along with the city. Long Beach was very young when my family arrived in 1890, just having started as a colony in 1882. The city's founder, William Willmore, visited Bessie's classroom in 1899 and spoke of the founding of the town. She remembered him as a poor, quiet, unhappy man. She introduced him as Mr. Willmore. He rose from his seat and told of the dream he had while standing on the corner of Anaheim and American, then just a dot on a large plain sloping toward north, east and west, with the ocean to the south. There he had envisioned a beautiful city on the bluffs overlooking a stunning sandy beach, with farmers settling on the rest of his colony. He shared his vision with a wealthy owner of a vast cattle ranch, Jotham Bixby. Mr. Bixby appreciated Willmore's dream and sold him 4000 acres of Bixby's Cerritos rancho. It was agreed that payments would be made out of the sale of lots and acreage of what Willmore called the American Colony.

Every colony had to have a townsite where people could shop and socialize. Mr. Willmore set aside 350 acres for his town which extended from the ocean to 10th Street and from where the Long Beach freeway is today to Alamitos Avenue. He named this town Willmore City. Lots in this new townsite sold from $25 ($684 in 2021) on up.

Father used to tell of a parcel at the corner of First and Pine, which became the site of the First National Bank building, purchased by a worker from the Rancho Los Alamitos for $50 ($1368 in 2021). The cowboy put down $10 ($273) and agreed to come back and pay the rest the next payday. He never came back and he lost his lot and a future fortune when downtown real estate began to boom.

Mr. Willmore's dream came true but the terms did not allow Mr. Willmore to profit by the dream, for he lost his entire interest in his enterprise. Mr. Willmore had been a man of his word and, as he had promised those who bought his town lots, used the money received to bring water and other amenities to his townsite. There was not enough left to pay Jotham Bixby.

Poor Mr. Willmore, unable to pay Jotham Bixby, was forced to sell his shares in the enterprise for $1. He left for Arizona, hoping to become involved in railroad building. Soon after the tiny town changed the name to Long Beach. I think this hurt the poor fellow more than the loss of his capital. He returned to Long Beach a poor, ill man and was forced to become an inmate of the Los Angeles County Poor Farm. He ran away and came back to Long Beach, where he lived in a tent, with no clothes except those on his back and a few cents to his name. Ida Crowe, a widow with seven children, took him in. Famers in the area, such as my parents, provided him with free produce to sell at a small fruit stand on Pine Avenue. It was only a few years later, in January 1901, that the dreamer was buried in an unmarked grave in the little city cemetery, not far from our home.

It becomes an even sadder story because had Mr. Willmore started his project two years later, or been able to hold on two years longer, he would have been a success. In 1885 the second transcontinental railroad was completed and a price war developed between it and the Southern Pacific. The result was a tremendous land boom in southern California, one which lured my parents westward. My sister Bessie was so touched by Mr. Willmore's story that she convinced a group of women, The Civic League of Signal Hill, to raise funds to put a headstone on his grave. This was accomplished in 1913.

Downtown and the Seashore

I'm glad I was born in Long Beach in the 1890s and grew up when horse and buggies were still in use. I remember the seven-mile-long beach which gave the city its name. There was a widely sloping beach below a tall bluff that tilted toward the west where farmers could drive wagons onto the white dry sand. Lavender verbenas and a yellow wild flower grew on the sand dunes. The beach was so wide you could drive a span of twenty horses, side by side, from the Los Angeles River to Alamitos Bay when the tide was low.

The Magnolia Pier was one of the chief attractions of the town when we moved to Long Beach in 1890. Built in 1885, mainly for fishing, it was at the foot of Magnolia Avenue and extended into the sea about 700 feet. But the weather and waves did deadly work. In February 1887, piles from the pier were driven ashore by a violent sea; though repaired, the pier gradually weakened. A new pier, the Pine Avenue Pier, was completed in May 1893 and the old Magnolia Pier was revitalized, with 200 feet added to the length. But heavy rains, high tides, and large ocean swells, damaged the old pier and in 1900, heavy swells swept away the remaining portion of the old wharf, also damaging the Pine Avenue Pier. In 1904, when I was 13, a "new" Pine Avenue Pier was built.

On Saturday, November 12, 1904, 50,000 people swarmed to Long Beach, according to newspaper accounts, to celebrate Pier Day, the opening of the new Pine Avenue Pier. The day began at sunrise with the raising of the flag at the end of the pier. This was followed by a gun salute from two Navy ships anchored offshore, which meant we had to gather our picnic lunch and get the buggy and ourselves ready quickly. We knew we had to be in town by 10 a.m. when a squad of mounted police led the parade from Locust Avenue to the pier. The mounted police must have left a lasting impression on 7-year-old Frank, who in later years joined the group.

We relished the music of the Long Beach Marine Band and various other marching bands from Santa Monica to Santa Ana who were part of the procession. We yelled and waved when we saw one of Bessie's students, Ella Wilson, crowned "Queen of the Ocean," riding on a float in front of three nautilus shells. In twin nautilus shells behind her were her maids of honor, Maude Walker and Lillie Kinman, who we also knew.

Later, there were speeches in Pacific Park. Governor Pardee started his speech with a slip of the tongue by saying "My friends of

Pasadena," but despite his guffaw he was presented with a golden key by the "Queen of the Ocean," our Pier Day Queen. At the front of the pier, a unique arch, christened the Gate of Neptune, was constructed with timber and piles from the old Pine Avenue Pier. With the key the governor ceremoniously proceeded to unlock the gate, declaring the pier open.

But my earliest memories go back to the late 1890s when there was a bathhouse, where bathing suits were rented for the day; the original Pine Avenue Pier, with a merry-go-round, food vendors and novelty shops; and a pavilion with twelve rooms including a large dining room and a dancehall surrounded by a balcony.

There were picnics on the beach, where the breakers rolled in upon the soft sands. Here hundreds of horses and buggies and many bathing machines (which we would call changing rooms today) had ample room, without crowding the frolicking children or hampering the grown-ups enjoying the band concerts. There weren't any paved roads into town and we went up hill and down many times via Atlantic Avenue. Once we reached the sea our horses were unharnessed and tied to the buggy with a sack of hay for lunch, joining the myriad of others at the east side of the Pine Avenue Pier.

The west side of the Pine Avenue Pier was reserved for bathers and picnickers. We always packed our own food for a picnic. Spending money to buy food for thirteen from vendors was something our family budget could not afford.

It was a real beach then and real surf but our parents forbid us to venture into the sea when the enormous green curls of powerful, towering waves thundered in. As we grew older, we would go out at night with a grown-up sister or brother as guardian to watch those same tremendous curls of force turn into fairyland lights when the phosphorous red algae bloomed. We could see fish swimming in that fascinating fluorescence and it was hard to leave the gorgeous display of nature with its magical colors.

If the tide was right, we could walk miles along the beach to Devil's Gate, just where the approach to the Belmont Pier now stands.

If not timed properly you could be caught with the incoming tide on one side and a sheer cliff on the other. Many failed to do this and had to be rescued by boat.

The beach was clean and the air clear and invigorating. We dug clams at will — little clams, razor clams and even the Pismo clam. Frolicking on the beach on summer days was a time to be relished in a family our size. There was always much boasting ahead of the trip about how deep we would venture into the ocean — "Up to my knee — up to my waist — up to my arm pits." But it was a different story when we met the sea with all its power and often a strong undertow.

From time to time one of us was overly courageous and misjudged the height and force of an oncoming wave. We got pounded to the sandy bottom and fought our way back up and out to the shore to recuperate on the beach and make a vow never do such a thing again.

I often bragged about how far I would go in the water, but I never lived up to my boast because I always got too cold. One day I was urged to go in deeper than I liked by some of my older siblings, who of course were taller and didn't feel they were too far out themselves. Bessie finally protested and said, "Leave Ivy alone. Let her go out on the sand and play if she wants to." Bessie took command and pulled me to the solitary sands of the beach where I could build castles, dig clams or just sit and watch the schools of porpoises pass by.

When I was about 6, I was busily building myself sand castles, paying no attention to my surroundings when I heard the trot of horses' feet close beside me. Someone was driving a pair of horses and a surrey at a rapid pace on the wet sand and didn't see me with my spade and shovel. Before the buggy wheels ran over me and knocked me unconscious, I remember that I saw horses' hooves above me. Thankfully, the horses had been careful and not stepped on me. The people in the buggy carried me into the dance pavilion and got hold of Mother, who was there when I regained consciousness. It frightened everyone else but me.

I loved the beach and looking for seashells. My sisters used to say I could have gone into the seashell business and made a fortune if I had been born a bit earlier and if Mr. Edward Eastman and his wife Fannie hadn't beat me to it.

When I asked the Eastmans about how they got started selling seashells they said it was merely good luck. Soon after they came to Long Beach from Chicago around 1896, they took a one-day sight-seeing cruise to Palos Verdes. It was on this trip the Eastmans first saw an abalone shell. Mr. Eastman and his wife were quite impressed by its size and the fact that such a shell could easily be made into strikingly beautiful jewelry. Telling his wife he was going to get another shell, she was astonished when her husband returned. He had purchased not one shell, but a ton of them! Mr. Eastman told his wife that if the shells pleased them, they would please others, so their new venture in California would be promoting abalone shells.

The abalones were being harvested by Japanese, who dived for them in the vicinity of White Point and Portuguese Bend, cutting them from the rocks. Their principal income from the abalones was through the sale of the meat. Little did they realize the value of the shell.

Soon the Eastmans opened a shell store on the north side of West Ocean Boulevard, east of the alley between Pine and Pacific. They had no previous knowledge about the shells, but the lovely abalone shells proved a popular novelty and the business thrived. The couple put in machinery for grinding shells and making jewelry, and the Japanese kept them supplied with abalone shells for years. The Eastmans later built the "Eastman Hotel" at Seaside Boulevard and Pier Place, and opened a shell store there. They also had a shell store for a time on the "new" Pine Avenue Pier, near the auditorium. Local abalone shells came to compose but one portion of the couple's greatly expanded business. Many other kinds of shells were imported from Japan, the South Seas and elsewhere.

I loved to visit their store, and could not help but remember what my sisters had teased me about. The Eastmans had no children, and I often fantasized about them adopting me and my eventually running the business. But then again, I wouldn't have traded Mother, Father and all my siblings for anything!

In the early days, the town was above the bluff. The city's first water tank was in a hollow on First Street, between Pine and Locust. The hollow helped generate sufficient pressure, or gravity flow, from the water supply farther north. The hollow also housed the city jail and Long Beach's first dog pound. At Locust and Broadway, the railroad tracks were so high above street level that people on opposite sides of Broadway couldn't see one another, and there was no way of getting across at that point.

The deep gully along Locust extended through and across First and Locust and to and across Ocean Boulevard. It had been filled in for the railroad track along Broadway, but the sidewalks along that street followed the dip of the gulch. If a person wanted to get from the south to the north side of Locust, they had to go either to American Avenue or Pine Avenue and then to Third Street and get around.

The first street above the beach was Ocean Avenue. Pine Avenue, leading north from Ocean, had a few shops. Driving into the "shopping district," which was approximately two blocks on Pine Avenue from Ocean Avenue to Second Street, was a real treat. I remember if we ever saw more than two or three other teams of horses on the streets besides our own on weekdays, we thought traffic was very heavy and something "special" had to be going on.

Mr. Boswell operated a general store; Mr. Holman had a drug store which also carried stationery and perfume; Mr. McCraken, who had the reputation as being the best bread maker in this part of the state, ran a bakery; and there was a livery stable run by the Fetherman family.

I remember the moments spent in front of Wingard's Pharmacy at First and Pine, drinking in the wonderful sights in the display window — the tall glass jars that in reality held only red, green and blue colored water but to me were rubies, emeralds and sapphires straight from fairyland, and Mr. Benefield who had a newsstand and stationary shop on Pine near the post office, where our mouth's watered trying to decide which candy we might buy with the money Father gave us for plucking the feathers off squabs for him to sell.

Our biggest treat was going to Mr. Parcel's where you could buy ice and ice cream sodas. His store on Ocean Avenue featured ice cream, soda water, and syrup. But slurping a fizzy beverage was considered inappropriate on Sunday, a day to honor God by going to church. So innovative people thought "just lose the soda." Presto — the ice cream Sunday was born. However, some thought it was wrong to name a dessert after the holiest day of the week, so the name was changed to ice cream sundae!

My older siblings often spoke of Mr. Dames, the proprietor of the Union Meat Market. I was too young to remember him, but they would regale me with stories of how Mr. Dames would fly into a rage if anyone handled meat or other articles on sale. He would frequently seize an offending patron by the ear, lead him to the door and order him to "get out and stay out." Today we would applaud such hygienic efforts, but then it was looked upon as rude. Father sold him chickens and squabs, and though Father never spoke ill of anyone, he did witness Mr. Dames become embroiled in numerous arguments which lost the butcher customers. I guess treating his clientele this way forced Mr. Dames out of business because he later moved from Long Beach. Years later, we overhead Father tell Mother that Mr. Dames had been murdered in Bellingham, Washington. Of course, at the word "murder" we were all ears! It seemed a screwdriver had been driven through his head.

One place we were told to stay away from was McCarthy's saloon at the northwest corner of Pine and Second. The saloon angered Father who thought he had moved to a temperance town. But after the town reincorporated in 1898, McCarthy was able to keep his license until it expired in July 1900 when the "good" people of Long Beach voted not to renew it.

It had been a difficult battle, because the one saloon was heavily taxed, enough to pay for city services. Now small farmers, business owners and land lords would have to pay a business tax. Though Father disliked taxes, he was pleased Long Beach would again be alcohol free, prohibited in any form except upon a physicians' prescription.

Pacific Park, today known as Lincoln Park, was a great place to visit. There we looked at the bones of the whale that washed ashore in 1897. The whale, which in later days was called "Minnie," even though it was a male, shared the whale house with Hannibal the eagle and Napoleon the peacock. There was also a lake that had real alligators.

The Countryside

I remember the floods we used to have before flood control was established in 1914. One of the greatest rainy seasons in regional history occurred when I was 18. On February 11, 1909, the San Gabriel River reached flood proportions, overflowing its banks. The river didn't flow into Alamitos Bay, like it does today. It joined the Los Angeles River on Rancho Los Cerritos land, creating a boggy area we called the Willows.

In the winter of 1909, a violent cascade of water swept down Pine and Pacific Avenues between State and Willow, continuing a headlong course down State Street (now Pacific Coast Hwy.) to Anaheim Street and the inner harbor. Streets in the northwest part of the city were impassable with water four feet deep. 1.71 inches of fell bringing the total rainfall for the season to-date to 13.90 inches. The previous year the total rainfall for the entire season was 10.04 inches.

The San Gabriel River became rampant about noon, when the flood waters in the foothills added to the stream. Soon the State Street Bridge was under water and unusable. Old timers could not remember a worst rainfall since we arrived in 1890, when inhabitants of North Long Beach went around in boats. The 1908-09 winter continued to be a wet one. By the end of March, the total rainfall for the season was over 18 inches.

The raging waters provided a good underground water level. Just north of Willow Street and west of American Avenue there was a swampy place called the Willows. This was a thicket of willow trees, interspersed with wild roses, a deep pink variety which Mother scorned because they were not the lovely pink and white ones she

43

had known in England. However, they made beautiful displays. There were also wild blackberries, which we would anxiously wait to ripen, our mouths watering at just the thought of such a tasty treat. Unfortunately the birds always seemed to get them before we did.

Tall primroses, with California poppies interspersed among grain fields, could be found along Willow Street. Many farmers raised apples and other fruit, like we did.

We often took an evening buggy ride along Willow to enjoy the blossoms and stop and say hello to our neighbors. Mother used to exchange recipes with some of the women, but Mother's apple pie, made in one of our large milk pans and served with Jersey crème couldn't be topped.

In times when it flooded farmers had to take row boats to save their farm animals. One enterprising real estate firm, after one or two dry years, when there had been no flood, cleared off land, laid out city lots and built houses to sell. The next year there were floods and water reached the window sills on the homes. Buyer beware!

There were also times when we had little rain. A period of drought followed the torrents of rain that greeted us when the family arrived in Long Beach in 1890. Though we had a well for water and irrigation, Father and other farmers were anxious for rain, fearful the underground water supply could dry up.

In April 1894 they decided to bring in a rainmaker, a Mr. Baker, from Visalia. Mr. Baker used dynamite to launch his "special" ingredients into the air. Why explosives? People had noticed that heavy rains usually fell soon after a battle, and surmised the rain was caused by the explosion of cannons and gunfire.

Mr. Baker launched his chemicals into the air and two or three times the barometer got down low enough for the rainmaker to tell customers that rain was coming. However, a week after he made this statement there was still no visible sign of rain. Baker claimed if he failed it would be the first time out of 16 trials that he did not produce rain.

The town decided to hire him for two more days because it did rain quite hard in Fullerton. Perhaps the prevailing winds from Long Beach had driven the rain clouds inland towards the foothills. Baker, who kept his formula a secret, did make it rain a little. Unfortunately, northerly winds quickly dried up the moisture from the soil. He collected his money claiming he produced about ¼ of an inch of rain for the town. He left in disgust because he said he couldn't do more with the winds against him.

Water is a valuable commodity in southern California, and William Penn Watson knew how to use it wisely. I remember the Watson family and how Mr. Watson attracted the attention of horticulturists all over the country by his successful experiments in dry farming. He believed that to water soil that could be farmed dry was an unpardonable sin. In 1888 Watson and his family moved to Long Beach from Linden, Washington, settling on a ranch at the corner of Willow and Perris Road (now Santa Fe Avenue). Father even paid a special visit into town to view the 61 pound, 2-foot-long sugar beet, and the 75-pound squash Mr. Watson had grown and put on display.

Then there was the General — Edward Bouton. Though I was only seven, I still remember the excitement over an artesian well he dug and going to see the "Big Bouton" in action.

In July 1898, the former Civil War general drilled an artesian well, just north of Carson and east of the Terminal Railway tracks, with astounding results. The well "ran wild" and formed what was to be known as Bouton Lake. When the unruly giant was capped, it still spouted a geyser 80 feet into the air from a two-inch pipe. When the sun's rays hit it right, the geyser-like column could be seen as far east as Whittier.

The railroad ran tourist trains from Los Angeles to view the huge water spout which many claimed was probably the greatest artesian well ever drilled anywhere in the world. Long before the well could be capped it had formed a lake, which extended more than a half mile in a northeasterly-southwesterly direction and was 500 feet wide. In 1899 Bouton entered into an agreement to furnish water to the city and by 1911 a large part of Bouton Lake had dried up. Today much of Lakewood sits atop what once was Bouton Lake.

Up until 1921 and the discovery of oil, much of what we now know as Long Beach and Signal Hill was farm land. Most new farmers to the area had to find outside employment for a year or two before their crops began to pay off. But Long Beach land was fertile. Locals said if a man had a horse, wagon and cultivating implements, he could, by crop rotation and proper irrigation, produce more on ten acres of Long Beach land than on forty acres east of the Rockies. Father had chosen well, but he had to watch his markets and anticipate what produce would be needed most and when. He also was careful to recycle everything into compost to be used as fertilizer. With such a large family we learned to be frugal.

Opportunities for farmers like Father continued to grow. I was 22 when a municipal market opened in downtown Long Beach in March 1913. The market movement was first launched by the Men's City Club in 1912. It never took off and was almost dropped when in January 1913 the Woman's City Club took up the fight to sponsor a civic project where farmers brought their produce to sell to the folks in town.

There was a great deal of publicity about this unique venture and competing store front merchants were not at all pleased about this unwelcome competition. Father decided to wait and see what developed.

On opening day there were sixteen stalls selling flowers, fruit, vegetables, poultry and eggs. Of course I had to be there, and I remember how customers were greeted by members of the Women's City Club who carried parasols and were dressed in colorful silk dresses. The market was a great success with every one of the stands selling out completely before closing time, probably because prices were 3 to 5 cents a pound less than what local markets were charging.

The market continued to grow, expanding to Tuesdays, Thursdays and Saturdays and including 140 stands, including one of ours.

Cucumbers were the mainstay of Signal Hill up until the time oil was discovered in 1921. A Japanese community grew up around us. Most leased land. I remember the fields of canvas the Japanese farmers placed over the cucumbers for protection. During the heat of the day, they would lift the edges of the canvas to provide ventilation. In late June the growers would roll up the canvas, since all danger of frost was past, and begin picking. During harvest, Japanese pickers would go through the fields with sacks capable of holding 40 pounds of cucumbers draped across their shoulders. A packing shed was set up at the edge of the field with Japanese women doing most of the packing, in addition to helping in field work.

In December 1918, a devastating fire hit Mr. Kiama's farm. The Japanese custom of using direct heat applied under the tub for heating bath water caused the tragedy. The floor of Mr. Kiama's home ignited. He was nearly trapped in the conflagration, but managed to escape from his home to call nearby neighbors for help. The flames from the house soon spread to other buildings, consuming three small cottages and a barn before the fire burned out. A fire was nothing compared to California's Alien Land Law of 1920, and the discovery of oil, which forced the Japanese off their fields, their farm leases not renewed.

Oil made many in our area rich, but not my family. In 1920, the area where our farm once stood was subdivided into a development called Atlantic Square. The subdivision was bounded by Atlantic Avenue, Pasadena Avenue, Perkins Street and 25th Street. All of the 142 lots were sold by December 1920, in a period of 90 days. Though the family made money in selling the land, things would have been different if we had waited a year. Like Mr. Willmore in establishing his city, our timing was off. Any oil discovered there was no longer ours to claim.

Growing up we loved to go for walks, roaming the hillsides and learning the habits of the birds, rabbits, coyotes and badgers. Bessie was our teacher and no better one could anyone wish for. She knew every wildflower and made our walks a real treat from start to finish.

The Los Angeles River flowed across Willow Street and American Avenue not far from our farm. During wet years there were forests of willow trees and wild roses. Hummingbirds made nests in the willows and red-winged blackbirds made their home in the tulles. In the early spring we watched for the orioles. I cannot remember whether it was the Bullock or the Arizona Hooded that arrived first. One built a long stocking of a nest in the eucalyptus trees. The other chose the fan palm for its swinging cradle. One year we were fascinated as we saw one bird on top of a broad fan and the other under a leaf. There they industrially passed the fibers of the leaves back and forth to one another to form a cradle in which to lay their eggs. We diligently went back every day to see if the young birds had hatched.

The orioles were the most colorful, though the little Audubon Warblers who loved our olive trees ran a close second when they stayed long enough to have their spring coloring. The warbler was a winter visitor but occasionally stayed long enough to show us his springtime beauty.

The linnet arrived about the same time as the orioles. The linnet loved to eat our fruit, but paid for it all by entertaining us with rollicking little songs. The sparrows were always with us as were mockingbirds and black birds. The swallows loved our barn and I remember climbing one of the rafters and carefully poking my fingers into a nest and feeling the eggs.

Perhaps my favorite bird was the meadow lark. There were many of them then, and I loved their musical call. A fence post seemed their favorite roost and we could easily get near enough to distinguish the shield on the breast.

The first note in the morning always appeared to come from the bee martin with his nest high in the big eucalyptus tree beside the house. He often seemed to call before daylight. He was not alone. One early spring morning, just after sunrise I looked into the orchard west of our home. There, coloring a row of apricot trees, perched a flock of migrating yellow headed blackbirds, all facing the rising sun. Really a golden glory.

I especially enjoyed migrating birds. There were bluebirds, whole flocks of them, rising in front of our approaching vehicle coming from town. Almost like a patch of the sky itself. The cedar wax wings visited us as well, but they gradually declined in number as the city grew and the countryside faded.

How we loved the quail, whose calls we tried to imitate. We had plenty of opportunity to practice since there were so many of them. Once running down a grassy slope on the other side of Atlantic Avenue I nearly stepped on a nest with eleven eggs. They were a little smaller than a hen's egg and delicately marked. Kathleen and I kept an excited watch on that nest but we never saw the babies.

Once a bee martin had its nest in a tall cypress tree and Edward convinced me to climb up and get two eggs for his collection. I put them in my mouth and climbing down I hit my chin on a branch and one egg broke. I knew I could not spit it out for fear of losing the second egg. It wasn't much fun carrying a broken egg in my mouth during my descent from the cypress tree, but Edward was very proud of me for doing it and earning his praise was worth it all.

There were two types of birds we didn't like — turkey buzzards and chicken hawks. One day someone shot a turkey buzzard and even dead it scared me. It was enormous and I'm not surprised that every winged creature would make a noise and run to hide when a turkey buzzard came into view.

Winter rains settled and smoothed out the dust in the streets, and we welcomed the green of spring which covered the land. How happy we were when spring vacation arrived and we had time to spend several days climbing Signal Hill. Judge Dillon had subdivided his 160 acres on Signal Hill into 20-acre parcels, but not all were sold or planted with crops, and we had the whole of nature to enjoy. We eagerly finished our household tasks and packed a picnic lunch. There was no need to bother with roads as there were fields over which we might walk. There were flowers everywhere, along the roadsides and in fields. We often stopped to pass the heavy lunch basket to another to carry which, once lunch was eaten, was perfect for carrying home wild flowers.

Our favorite spot was the brow on the north side of Signal Hill, where acres of yellow violets peeked through the tall green grass. One of our favorite activities was rolling down the grass hill. Up and down the slope we went, neglectful of the grass stains Mother would need to launder out. Exhausted by our play, as well as our long walk, the lunch long ago consumed, we took the string we had brought to tie the bunches of wildflowers we gathered on our way home.

We avoided the south side of Signal Hill with its beds of cactus, but elsewhere we found other wild flowers — rabbit ears, brodea, sun cups and many others to add to the basket. The west side of Signal Hill had a few canyons. Fern canyon was damp and shady and grew tiny gold back or silver back ferns. We usually dug out a few of these but did not have much luck in growing them at home. At the foot of the hill, we searched eagerly among the brush for the fragile baby blue eyes which we wrapped in moss so they would survive the walk home.

During the wonderful week of spring vacation, we took many short trips to what we called the Hill, making sure we went there on Saturday before school started to pick wild flowers to take to our teachers on Monday when our holiday was over.

Sometimes we would venture further afield and visit Palos Verdes, so green in the spring. In the late afternoon its deep ravines made lovely shadows against its amethyst color. As the sun set over its hills, beautiful colors emerged, made more brilliant with masses of clouds. Then the moon would appear and the dazzling stars. Yes, we could see the stars then, before the town and city lights shut them from our view.

I remember one year a group of us took a boat to San Pedro and from the water front climbed to the top of Palos Verdes. A foggy morning had left the tall malva leaves full of water and we became drenched as we scrambled through them. But the view from the top made it all worthwhile. The sun pushed the fog away and we looked back across San Pedro Bay to Saddleback Mountain, then to the stretch of ocean, to Catalina with the other Channel Islands in the distance. We marveled at Mount Baldy, covered in a white, glistening snow. A brisk wind began to blow which dried off our wet clothes. What a day it had been! The wild flowers were beautiful as well as the Mariposa lilies, which we did not find on Signal Hill.

The eucalyptus trees were a much-loved childhood associate. One long row of eucalyptuses stretched from Willow Street down to the beginning of the Saunders' place, then turned west to American Avenue. There was another row that ran along the west side of our five acres to the Shrode place. There was one break on the east side that permitted a low cypress hedge in front of our garden and a roadway into our yard north of the ranch house.

We had one big eucalyptus tree beside the house. We loved the old tree and marveled at the girth of its huge trunk. It was very old and Father was always concerned that a limb might break off and fall on the roof. When a branch grew big and looked as if it might be too brittle to withstand a storm, Father would tie a rope around it, cut it partly through, and rig up a block and tackle to see that its fall caused no damage during a storm.

I reveled in the grace and beauty of that old eucalyptus. I loved the laborious climb to the tuft of foliage at the top where the eucalyptus leaves were thick enough to hide me. I would sit in seclusion, in my special place, with a book to read and an apple to munch on. At night I could see other eucalyptus trees from my bedroom window, a row of them marking the boundary line between our place and the Shrodes. I relished watching the eucalyptuses on moonlit nights but even more I loved when a windy rain storm sent them bowing and scraping towards one another, the turbulence and the noise of the wind and rain lulling me to sleep.

They were useful trees. The new growth of leaves on the young eucalyptuses' sprouts made lovely writing paper. The old, dry, hard pointed leaves were used to make hats and baskets. The small twigs that fell to the ground provided kindling for our wood stoves, the best fuel we could find.

There were many other trees as well. We had a splendid orchard with many different fruits, fine for a family of hungry children. Across Atlantic Avenue our neighbor had planted a row of tall cypress trees and there we found many bird nests.

But it was the eucalyptus I loved most. It was my refuge when family stress seemed too much for me and I fled to the row at the end of the farm to throw myself on the ground until my spell of weeping was over. The eucalyptus was my friend, and a good listener. Whenever I see a eucalyptus today, I remember the calming influence it provided. It still brings great joy and memories.

Magnolia Avenue Pier c. 1885.
Courtesy of the Long Beach History Collection, Long Beach Public Library

Opening day of the Pine Avenue Pier in 1893. It would be
replaced by the "New" Pine Avenue Pier in 1904.
Courtesy Historical Society of Long Beach

Ocean Boulevard and Pacific Park, c1902.
Courtesy Historical Society of Long Beach

Sunday at Long Beach, c 1900.
Courtesy of the Long Beach History Collection, Long Beach Public Library

Picnic on Signal Hill, c1915.
Courtesy Historical Society of Long Beach

AT HOME

The Pacific Squab and Poultry Farm

I'm not sure when Father bought the five acres out of town, on Atlantic near Twenty-fifth Street, though I am sure it was just a year or so after we arrived. It came furnished with many things — a horse, a cow, farm equipment, a wagon shed, some furniture in the house, as well as a fruit orchard with apple, apricot, orange, walnut, peach and plum trees. There were also blackberries, raspberries, strawberries and a vineyard. Here, on what came to be called the Pacific Squab and Poultry Farm, the family raised 2,000 chickens, 5,000 pigeons and squabs (young pigeons), 10 cows, and 12 pigs.

Raising squabs was more difficult than raising chickens, since the baby pigeons were essentially helpless as newborns. They had to be in close proximity to their parents and given a great deal of attention. This reduced the number of offspring most pigeons were able to have.

Squabs were usually "harvested" for their meat when they were under four weeks old. The meat had a slightly gamey flavor, and tasted more like duck than chicken. Their meat was very tender since they came from birds that never flew.

One of our chores was to pluck the feathers off the squabs before Father sold the birds to local meat markets, hotels and restaurants.

We learned that squab was considered a delicacy, which meant Father could get a higher price for them than chicken.

My sister Bessie, always the teacher, told us squabs were domesticated before chickens and said to have first been eaten in ancient Egypt.

The cows terrified me until Daisy, our Jersey cow, looked at me with her beautiful brown eyes. I knew then that Daisy loved me. I showed her my love by taking her bits of cauliflower, carrots and apples. She appreciated the treats I brought and when I had to lead her somewhere she lowered her horns so I could easily reach one and guide her. This was fine for me but one day I was sick in bed and Norah was asked to bring Daisy in from the pasture. Norah came back in tears and without Daisy. She said every time she went near Daisy, Daisy tried to hook her. Then Anne was sent and she too came back in tears and no Daisy. When I heard this, I laughed and told them Daisy only wanted to make it easy for them by lowering her head so they could easily reach a horn. My sisters quickly learned that a bowing of the head did not mean an attack.

We had a barn. It was old, of the type that was tall in the center to accommodate a loft, with a stable on the south side and a wagon shed on the north. There were big double doors for the lower part and more for the top. One third of the barn was for the hay.

This was our playground, our gymnasium, also a good place to find a nook in which to curl up with a good book and feast on fruit from the orchard. We would climb the beams to the top most peak of the barn roof. Below us there might be plenty of hay if it was winter, or a scant portion in the spring. I was brave enough to try the climb when there was plenty of hay below. Once I let myself drop.

Oh, what fear and breathlessness as I sped through the air and landed flat on my back on the hay! I must admit that one jump was enough for me, though I would still climb to the roof and explore.

A third of the barn was what we called the "wagon lodge" and there were buggies and a two-horse wagon. We used to climb into a buggy or wagon and imagine them taking us to faraway places.

A barn was where there was hay for hens to hide away a stolen nest and raise her own family to her heart's content. A barn was where oats and barley bins existed for horse feed. All these temptations meant rats! Where did they live? In peace and quiet below the huge old barn. Once I crawled under the barn to find where a hen had made a nest. It was dark and all I could think about was running into rats and the possibility of never being able to crawl back out and see my family again. I never found the hen's nest because my fear drove me back to the light of the sun, illuminating my way to the small hole where I had so bravely crawled in.

Of all the fun we had in our old barn nothing provided more excitement than the occasional rat chase. Having rats meant that every few months we had to tackle the increased rat population, for they grew in numbers faster than rat traps or cats exterminated them.

On rat gathering day each of us children came armed with a handy piece of wood which we never used, but held in self-defense. Four or five men would run about and turn our big fire hose on under the barn. A bulldog, our Airedale and a bird dog assisted in the battle. As the rats were routed with the force of the water they came running out and headed for a big wood pile on the other side of the driveway, the dogs chasing them. We all screamed because we always expected the fleeing rats would attack us or seek protection from the dogs by hiding under the folds of our skirts! Fortunately for us, our terrified shrieks seemed to work in scaring them off.

I often wondered who was the most frightened during the melee, the rats or the screeching child. Goodness knows we were too petrified to have tried to use our wooden bat to deter them. If you think I am exaggerating about a rat running up your skirt, I have to tell you one of the rats did run up one man's trouser leg. Being an adult, he didn't scream, which would have been an effective weapon. Instead, he did a Highland fling and tossed the rat away. The whole rat episode produced nightmares for many of us, but would we miss it? Never!

We children had fun naming the farm animals and sometimes went far afield to find a new name. Someone took a trip on a ship called *Coos Bay* and a visiting friend said she always wondered why our little three colored kitten always made her feel seasick until she heard one of us call the kitten Coos Bay.

We even borrowed names from our history books. One unfortunate calf was named Poppea Sabina for Nero's wife who Nero killed by kicking the pregnant woman in the stomach when she complained he spent too much time at the races. My brother Tom thought it was no wonder that our calf seemed to have mental troubles with such a name.

Then there was our horse Tommy, who was rather small, a plodder, quiet. No, he wasn't named for my brother, Tom. He already had the name when we got him. He liked to watch us with his strangely placid eyes, perhaps plotting his next surprise. He was used mainly for plowing, but was harnessed to the light farm wagon when we needed to do shopping in town or to take us to church on Sunday. When he wasn't needed for those duties, he would take four of my sisters to high school.

My sisters usually walked to high school at Eighth and American, though Father made Tommy more available during the winter months. On cold days my sisters stayed in bed as late as possible, snuggling under the warm blankets, quickly dressing and making their way to the warm kitchen to start the day.

Anxious not to be late for school, they always tried to make Tommy hurry. Josie usually held the reins, with Helen, Norah and Anne sitting nearby. In spite of the fact that they wore out several whips on him, Tommy trudged along at his own rate of speed most of the time.

Josie told me of the time they picked up a neighbor on the way to school and a horsefly bit Tommy. Away he went! Hats flew off, for all girls wore hats to school in those days. Josie stood up and slapped Tommy with the reins; losing her balance, she fell behind old Tommy. Helen climbed out on the shaft of the wagon and retrieved the reins, but a wheel went over Josie, leaving her black and blue. Helen finally got Tommy to calm down and turned around to pick up Josie and her precious yellow hat, now ruined, lying in the road.

Tommy generally obeyed, but once in a while he decided he was in control, usually on the way home and more often on a day when rain was in the air and perhaps falling. His ears would go up, in fact his whole head, and he would change his gait and charge ahead with his tail circling about. Josie and the others would scream "whoa" at the top of their lungs, Josie pulling on the reins with all her might. Then, just as suddenly, he would drop back into his usual slow trot.

Sometimes after school my sisters would be given errands to do downtown. Once when they went to the butcher on Pine Avenue Josie forgot to tether Tommy firmly to the horse rail. Tommy ran away, much to their distress and the amusement of bystanders. Another time Josie had to make a noon hour trip to Third and Olive where my brother Tom's mill was. Helen went with her and on the way there, Tommy ran away! The usual screaming followed, alerting the onlookers. Suddenly Tommy stopped and leaned down to eat grass by the side of the road as if nothing had happened. This part of his misbehavior was always most irritating. It was as if he had orchestrated the whole thing just for his own amusement.

One Saturday Mrs. Neece, a neighbor, asked us if we wanted to go to the peat bogs near Compton where we would find wild violets. Since her buggy could only hold two, we used our wagon with Tommy at the helm. We had a grand time and picked plenty of long-stemmed purple violets and started home along a path next to the railroad track. Driving happily along, we were enjoying our trip when someone glanced back and saw a train approaching. We were terrified. There was not enough room for our large wagon and a train to pass. There were fences everywhere which meant there were few places where we could pull over. What if the train blew its whistle? We knew Tommy hated train whistles. We spotted a space that might be big enough for us to fit. We tried to hurry Tommy but he jogged placidly along. Suddenly, the train did whistle a long toot. Up went Tommy's ears and away he went, all of us yelling at him to stop. Mrs. Neece and her passenger were behind us. Their buggy was small enough that it didn't need to pull over for the train. I can imagine how they laughed at the sight. Yes, laughed, for when Tommy reached that open space he quickly stopped and happily bent down and began to enjoy a meal of fresh spring grass.

Yes, Tommy had personality. One day my brother Edward led him into the stable and put the plow harness on him. When they finished Tommy decided he needed a good run. Tommy suddenly wheeled around and away he went, head up and tail waving, across the yard, out the drive and away down Atlantic Avenue. I do not remember who found him later, standing meekly beside the hitching post of the Episcopal church, Pickles' Hall, on Third and Atlantic. A place he took us to every Sunday. What a memory he must have had.

I wonder how I would feel now if I could just go into my back yard and hitch up old Tommy and drive down Pasadena Avenue. I can imagine how I would laugh and how Mother would smile as I drove by, encouraging old Tommy to go as fast as he could, kicking up his heels.

We had another horse, whose name escapes me. One day Caroline, Ethel, Anne and I took the buggy into town to shop on Pine Avenue. There was a hitching rail midway between Ocean Avenue and First Street and as Caroline drove up she forgot all about this horse not liking to be tied. As she slipped the rope around the rail, the horse reared in protest and caught Caroline's thumb between the rope and the rail, ripping the top of her thumb off to the base of the nail. Fortunately, the doctor's office was in the building just across the street.

The barn and the animals were a great source of fun and enjoyment. We always had at least one dog. Our favorites were old Vic, part Newfoundland and part St. Bernard. She would let any child romp with her and never snapped at us or even growled unless we were too rambunctious. Then there was Fay, Mother's little pug.

Walking home from school, our first sight would be Mother seated by the window darning stockings and Fay perched in the window sill with her front paws on Mother's lap. Fay was never far from Mother's skirts. Wherever she went, there was Fay, her head just under the edge of Mother's skirt back and forth — table to stove — stove to sink — indoors or outdoors Fay was there following each step Mother made. Then one day Mother fell ill and was too sick for Fay to come in the room. It was a lengthy illness and Fay pined for the sight of her. Every one that came or went through that bedroom door saw a pathetic little pug dog lying outside the door raise her head hopefully and then put it down again.

The day came when Mother was better and Fay was allowed in. She leapt on the bed, licked Mother's pale hands and then, knowing somehow that she must be gentle with her, showed her joy by going over the bed and under the bed and over the bed and under the bed until someone stopped her. The pug then went round the room like a whirling dervish. When that became too much for poor Mother, Fay was quickly pursued, somehow grabbed, and taken out of the room. However, Fay's excitement still knew no bounds. Exiled outdoors, she ran around the house again and again, then widened her perimeter to encompass the fruit orchard. It seemed there was no end in expressing her delight that Mother was better. We were afraid Fay would have a heart attack. But no, she finally came back indoors and lay once more outside Mother's door. She seemed to know all was well. Perhaps she had thought she would never see Mother again.

One winter evening a man appeared at our back door wanting to know if we wanted to buy the two tiny animals he carried in his arms. We were all eyes and ears as Tom bargained for the animals with beautifully marked striping on their heads. No — they were not skunks — they were badgers. The mother had been killed by a Pacific Electric car not far from us, leaving her offspring alone to die. The man evidently knew that among all the children in the Harnett family at least one would have an excess of motherly love and take on the care and feeding of two baby badgers.

It wasn't just one of us who fell in love with the baby badgers, which we named Mutt and Jeff, but all of us! We would take turns at hourly bottle feeding 24-hours a day. They won our hearts. Once one stopped feeding, the other poor little fellow began crying. It was so heartbreaking. We diligently took turns feeding but, even with our dedication, Jeff died after a ten-day battle.

Mutt grew to manhood, with claws two inches long on his front legs that were strong enough and quick enough to dig a hole so quickly it would make one dizzy. When a chicken, pigeon or rabbit died, we didn't eat them, we buried them. Generally, the meat spoils very rapidly and we didn't know exactly when the animal died or what was the cause of death. Mutt didn't care about spoiled meat. He loved the smell of a buried chicken, which he would speedily dig up. To us the odor was putrid and offensive, but to Mutt it was the smell of heaven, making him drool. He resurrected a rabbit one Sunday afternoon when we took a friend to the back yard to show off our dear little pet badger. We lifted Mutt out of the huge barrel, ½ full of dirt which was his home. We placed him on the ground and before we knew what was happening, he had exhumed a long dead, stinking rabbit and laid it as a welcoming gift, at the feet of our dainty friend.

Canning

Coming from a damp English climate, it took us awhile to adjust to the warm, hot summers of southern California. But the warmth and sun ripened the fruit on our trees.

Our summer mornings were busy times when fruit was ripe. Father would bring in the lovely ripe peaches and assign each of us a chore. We younger Harnetts were taught to peel peaches very carefully. "Waste not, want not" was our motto. Teenage sisters helped cook the fruit and put it into the two-quart mason jars. Even three-year-old Frank was assigned a task — keeping the wood box full.

There were other days when we made jam. Besides the peaches there were big black figs, and apricots. We liked the apricots, because they did not have to be peeled, only halved and the stones removed. The kitchen was warm so we sat on the wide back porch to peel the fruit, but poor Bessie had to stand by the hot stove to fill the jars and screw on the lids. By noon, there was ample proof of our labors.

During the hot afternoons we rested or played. After a good noon dinner, perhaps cold sliced meat from the Sunday roast with plenty of fresh vegetables from the garden and apple pie to finish off, Mother and baby Frank retired for naps and the rest of us younger ones were sent to the big cool barn or out under the trees to play. The big pepper tree was a favorite place of entertainment. We even parceled it out so that each child could claim a big rough branch as their own. The barn was fairly cool and a good place to read a book before it was filled with hay.

Yes, summers had their good points and it was not too many years before we were enjoying the warmth that had seemed so unpleasant in the beginning.

Our "Modern" Conveniences

When Father bought the five acres out in the country north of Long Beach at 25th and Atlantic there was a house which had little in the way of modern improvements. There was no sewer and we had to use an outhouse in the back yard. We weren't alone, even downtown folk had to have outdoor privies.

The sewage problem became troublesome when the town started to grow after the arrival of the Pacific Electric in 1902. My brother Tom's milling company was right next to the Long Beach Steam Laundry at Olive and Third. Though the laundry had cesspits they began to back up and smell. People began to worry about a possible epidemic caused by poor drainage, and passed a bond to build a big redwood septic tank for the town. The system, said to be the largest in southern California, capable of handling the sewage of a town of 30,000 was built and operating by 1904. I was thirteen then, and thought it a marvelous improvement to the town, however, problems with tree roots and flooding quickly quelled my enthusiasm. Finally in 1914 another bond measure passed, which even allowed us farmers to hook up to the sewage system. By then people knew that a good sewer system was essential to public health.

When we wanted to bathe, before we had "modern" improvements, we used a round wash tub with water heated on top of the stove. During warm weather, bathing was done in a bedroom but in the winter the kitchen was more popular, kept cozy with a good hot wood fire nearby.

Saturday was tub time in the Harnett household. The younger ones were bathed first and water was not changed too often until the older ones became fussy and demanded clean water. The last one in had to be sure the tub was emptied and put away, although if the last bather decided to wait until morning to do so, there could be consequences.

Such was the case when Father got up one evening when he heard one of us having a nightmare. He fell over the tub of water, reached for something to save himself, pulled the handle of the drawer full of table silver and crashed the whole thing to the floor. Pretty noisy for a while!

Such was the situation for seven years. Then my brother Jack, who had stayed in England to finish his education, joined us in Long Beach. We still had no bath tub until he built us one. Perhaps his engineering studies helped. He used heavy boards, six feet long, with a lining of zinc neatly sloped at one end and well joined. His creation was about two feet deep. We used five-gallon coal oil cans to heat enough water. Fortunately, the cans had handles, because they were quite heavy when full. It was fun to fill this tub and to put two or three little folks in at a time.

Next came the problem of emptying the tub whose usual place was standing on end in the corner of the kitchen. Jack cut a round hole in the kitchen wall near the floor. The garden hose was then brought in through the hole. One child stood outside holding the top of the hose high while the child in the kitchen waited to fill the hose with bath water. Then came the crucial moment when the child in the kitchen plunged the end of the hose into the water, called to the other who lowered his end to let the water run away. That was much easier than using a bucket to empty the tub. One "hurry-up" way was to hold the indoor end in the dirty water while the child outside sucked the hose. You had to be careful to listen to the gurgling of water in the hose and drop the hose quickly or else you would be rewarded with a mouthful of dirty water!

Yes, it was better than the wash tubs, but what a wonderful thing it was when we had sewage and built on a bathroom with a proper tub and other modern plumbing. There were still a lot of us around and it used to amuse our guests to see the long row of hooks along the wall, each with a name above it and a towel hanging on it. Saved a lot of confusion.

What did we use on our floors? Rugs, of course, but only in some rooms. Straw matting was a new idea that worked well in the bedrooms. The kitchen was bare wood. Then someone invented linoleum and what a help that was. I remember the elaborate window exhibit at Finney and Young in downtown Long Beach. It described how linoleum was made, showed different colors to choose from, told how you could have a linoleum rug, which you could pull up and take with you if you moved, or have it permanently attached to your floor. We were all overjoyed when our kitchen was covered with this new product, which was a joy to clean, compared to the old wood floor, which, though clean, was full of grease spots.

For washing laundry, we used a wooden tub with paddles in it. The paddles were turned by a wooden handle on top of the lid. Father was the best at operating the contraption, having more strength than the rest of us to move it vigorously back and forth. It really worked quite well.

Laundry wasn't the only thing we churned. We made our own butter – yes, real butter made from thick Jersey cream. We had a round wooden churn with a handle on the side to turn the paddles inside. Simple enough if the temperature was right. Sometimes, it took a long time for the butter to separate from the buttermilk, but when it was done how good it was.

We cooked on a wood stove. We enjoyed the heat in winter, but not so much in summer. Eucalyptus was the best wood. There were eucalyptus groves in various parts of the community that sold this wood by the cord.

Did you ever make toast over red hot coals? No toaster toast can ever rival that flavor, especially with home baked bread. Baking was an art, for we had no controlled heat. One of us always had to be on hand to add more wood to get the right temperature. I remember how we had to clean away the ashes and decide where they must be put on the farm to do good and no harm. We did find that the ashes were useful in shining our steel knives, scouring pots and pans and keeping the stove shining clean.

For cleaning the house, we used a broom and a mop. Down on one's knees was the best way to mop. Vacuum cleaners were still not invented. We did not even have many different cleaning solutions to put on the dust cloths, a little vinegar or coal oil when we wanted to clean the windows. Yes, one does have an easier time cleaning house these days.

At first, we did not have refrigeration, though we did buy a block of ice once in a while. Father built us a cooler, a frame work encased in screening with several shelves inside, which we kept in the shade of the eucalyptus trees. On the shelves we placed pans of milk which kept the milk nice and cool. We could skim the cream from the milk to make butter which, during summer months, we kept in the cooler along with eggs. To protect items stored in the cooler from ants, we would place the legs of the cooler in cans of water.

The invention of the telephone was a great help to farmers. We were two miles away from a large grocery store. When our phone was installed, we were able to telephone for groceries instead of driving the horse and buggy to town for them. Also, we could talk to friends in other parts of the community, that is, unless their phone happened to be on the other company's line.

Yes, there were two phone companies in Long Beach that I remember — Home and Pacific. The first phone company was actually Sunset, which was established in 1896, when I was still a toddler. It eventually sold its holdings to Pacific. Home had been around since 1904. Fortunately for us, my brother Tom had a feed business and had both telephone company's phones installed, so we could at least relay a message through him if it was important. Later we installed both phone company phones ourselves, as did a number of people. However, it was not long before the two companies were bought by a larger firm and combined.

Not all people had phones. One neighbor, who earned a living for herself and her invalid mother by giving music lessons, used to use our phone to make and receive calls. That meant one of us had to go to her house, a short block away, to call her to the phone. We did not particularly mind since there was usually someone able to go after her, but we were surprised to learn that the business cards she gave to her pupils had our number printed on them — as if the telephone was in her own home!

Our home number was Pacific 27, and the Long Beach Milling Company, my brother Tom's business, was Home 13, a very different look from the ten-digit numbers of today. When they reached four digits, it was fun for youngsters to phone a friend on New Year's Day and say "Is this 1923" and tell the one who said no, to tell him to look again at his calendar. Yes, those early phones were fun as well as convenient. Still fun, I guess. My teen age niece when I remonstrated her about a long conversation on one, replied "But Aunt Ivy, I am a teenager."

Sharing Germs

Yes, all of us shared not only a mother and father but any ailments that were going around.

When the measles hit, Bessie was the first to break out in a rash. Then the measles spread to us young folk — Kathleen, Frank and myself. We were very sick and were put in the "Children's Ward," while Bessie, whose bedroom adjoined the ward, lay recuperating trying to give us a word of cheer from her darkened room to ours.

When Mother and Father could spare moments, they read to us. No one else was allowed beyond the formaldehyde curtain hanging outside our door. Frank always begged to be read *Ric-a-tick-a-tavi,* a short story in the 1894 anthology *The Jungle Book* by Rudyard Kipling, about adventures of a valiant young Indian grey mongoose. Father furthered his interest by telling how Father's sister-in-law Helen Roby Harnett, who had married Father's brother Alfred, had been born in Bengal, India. I can only imagine how that added to Frank's fascination with the faraway land. Kathleen and I listened to *Ric-a-tick-a-tavi* whenever it was his choice to pick the reading material, though after hearing it so many times we pressured him to choose something different.

Kathleen and I both loved *Ministering Children*, by Maria Louisa Charlesworth, about how both rich and poor children helped those in need. The book inspired us so much I remember how after we recovered we recruited neighborhood children into forming our own "Ministering Children's League." We made badges and on Sunday afternoons put on sanctimonious airs as we took fresh strawberries to people too sick to leave their homes. I'm sure we must have been ghastly bores, trying to act as righteous as the children in the book, when normally we would have been funny and given the ill something to laugh at.

As if measles weren't enough, mumps hit the family in 1907. Kathleen was the first, bringing them home from school. Her case was so mild no one realized she had them before everyone in the family was exposed. There were ten of us who finally succumbed and we were a sad lot. Helen, who was a cashier at the Wise Company, and teachers Norah and Josie left home immediately when they heard the word "mumps." Tragically, they came home one by one to join the rest of the Mumps Brigade. Caroline won the honor of having the most interesting mump. It was one solid mump – huge – extending from cheek bone to shoulder.

Kathleen continued to only have a mild case, and one day when Dr. Harvey visited the Mumps Brigade he was horrified to find her out wading in an irrigation ditch looking for turtles. Poor Bessie, however, had far reaching complications that affected her eyes and she was advised to take a year's leave of absence from her post as head of the History Department at Long Beach High School. She often sat at the piano, her eyes blindfolded, playing everything she had memorized. After months of recuperation at home, she set sail for England, sufficiently recovered. Preparations were vast. She even packed a live horned toad in her suitcase and created quite a stir among our relatives who had never seen anything like it before. Gradually, her strength and health returned.

Visitors

Sunday afternoons friends came to call and it was not unusual for five or six guests to stay for supper. Mother would whip up a batch of English muffins baked in our wood burning oven. The muffins went well with the cans of sardines we always kept on hand and the bowls of strawberry preserves and marmalade.

With twenty or more at the table the conversations varied and frequently there were several going on at once, making for a noisy dinner. Anne was away in Pasadena a great deal — first attending Throop Polytechnic Institute for her art degree and later the Batchelder Tile Company where she was a modeler and designer. When she came home on weekends she began to understand why guests were often bewildered by our unconventional dinner conversations.

In "polite" society one conversation at a time was acceptable practice. We believed ourselves to be "polite" and debated the cause for our impoliteness. We decided our red wallpaper might have had something to do with it. Perhaps the red color made us more boisterous and argumentative. We decided to change the wallpaper to a lovely scene of trees and flowers — no red ones. No difference, our table talk continued to be energetic and lively!

But having multiple conversations, loud voices, and other dinner distractions proved a boon to me in later years. I realized this in an English class my sophomore year of high school. The room was divided in half, one side trying to write a poem or story while the other half went about trying to engage the writers in loud conversation, even banging on desks to keep us from concentrating on our assignment. It was supposed to be a lesson on keeping quiet when coursework was done in the classroom and how students needed quiet to concentrate on an assignment. To the amazement of all I was not the least disturbed by all the racket. I had learned to "tune out" the din around me from our "unconventional" dinners.

Another time my poem "The Storm," published in our high school annual, Caerulea, and the best poem of my life (you'll find it at the end of this book), was written at our noisy dining table, which after the meal and the mountains of washed dishes became a study table for our homework. It was a noisy affair with someone conjugating French or Latin verbs, someone else hearing another's spelling for the next day, and still several others arguing over assignments.

One distant cousin whose family settled in Canada and later moved to San Francisco was Ned Bolger. Ned was a city lad and came every other summer to stay for a few weeks. He was quite handsome and most of the girls in the family had a crush on him. He teased us and we in turn teased him.

One 4th of July he dunked Anne and Josie in the ocean, much to their dismay. They decided to get even with him. Ned was to leave on an early train for San Francisco the next morning. For revenge they planned to wake him, and hopefully frighten him out of his wits, by lighting giant fire crackers they had saved from the previous day. Josie and Anne even recruited us younger ones and we were all for it.

At four thirty in the morning all were ready for the bombardment. At a signal from Frank all the firecrackers were lit and the sound they made was deafening. We had warned Mother and Father what we planned so they wouldn't be frightened, but neglected to tell our three dogs whose excited barking added to the general uproar. Not a sound came from Ned's room and when Father woke him up at 5 a.m. he made it seem that he had not heard the furious firecracker assault. We were sure he was bluffing, but Ned refused to give us the satisfaction of knowing that it frightened, or even woke him. He even criticized us for an untidy hall and bathroom — littered with the mess from the firecrackers.

Two years later when Kathleen was having dinner with Ned and his mother, Cousin Mary, he accidently mentioned something about the explosions. Kathleen exclaimed, "Then you did hear it." He laughingly said he had heard me say "I wonder if his heart is O.K." and Kathleen saying "We'll take the blame." He never liked to let us think we ever put anything over on him, ever.

Being an only child, he was used to getting his own way. He prided himself on his intellect and would rarely admit defeat. One "discussion" with Ned was when he told of water being a conductor of electricity. I spoke up and said "not pure H2O. It is the particles in the water that conduct." He vehemently disagreed with me and when I told him I would show him my laboratory experiment book from our chemistry course in high school, he said no picayunish experiment could prove him wrong. He needed to be in Los Angeles the next day and said he would see an electrical engineer so he would have support against my "ignorant" claim. That night at dinner he came as close as he ever did in all of his visits with us to admitting ignorance. He really did not want to talk about the subject but of course we teased him with it even further until he finally admitted he had learned we were "partly" right and he was "partly wrong."

Ivy's Scars

I have many fond memories of the good times we had at our ranch and the surrounding countryside. However, the days at 2489 Atlantic Avenue were not all just fun, though we had fun most of the time, sometimes we got into trouble. I have the scars to prove it!

One dark winter morning after breakfast, my sister Helen wanted someone to go outdoors with her and play on the see-saw. It was almost time for her and my older sisters to be washing the breakfast dishes and tidying the kitchen before packing lunches for school. No one seemed to have time for play so Helen took me, one of the "small fries." Because she was so much bigger it was an uneven match. When she teetered down and I was way up in the air, she hit the ground so hard it knocked me off my seat and I fell, my poor chin losing all its skin and more!

Helen carried me, weeping, indoors. While Mother took care of my poor chin, my oldest sister, Bessie, brought me the whole end of a cake, covered with caramel icing. She knew I was very fond of caramel icing and it did the trick. I stopped crying. I often think of that luscious piece of cake when I look at the scar that still remains.

Another morning my brother Edward and I were playing cops and robbers, or some such game, and he was chasing me. He was a good bit older and could out run me, so I dashed into the big barn and slammed the door shut before he could get to me. I slipped the wooden bar into place to lock the door and peeked out through a knot to see where Edward was. Not seeing him anywhere around and thinking he had given up the chase, I unbarred the big door to have a good look and opened it wide enough to get my little head out – just in time to get hit by a log. Poor Edward. My forehead bled and bled and he was so afraid he'd get punished for throwing the log at me! He had only meant it to hit the barn door and scare me. That's another of the many scars I can tell you stories about!

When neighbors visited, they often brought their children with them. One family came to play baseball each Saturday afternoon. We had a lot of fun, though there were days when we got into a fight over the umpire's decision and the young ball players went home vowing they were never coming again. BUT they returned the next Saturday, eager to have another game!

Friends coming and going with horses and buggies were a temptation to little girls and boys. One thing we used to do was hang on the back of the buggy and run along behind as the horse sped away. We would then let go when our little legs could no longer keep up. Of course, we were forbidden to do this. It was too dangerous. But we did it anyway!

One afternoon some of the Dillon family, who lived on their big ranch on Signal Hill, came to see us. As they were about to drive home, several grown up Harnetts gathered around the buggy to say "good-bye." The Dillons did not know I was hiding behind my mother and older sisters, concealed by their long, full, ruffled skirts. I figured this was my chance. I got hold of the back of the Dillon's buggy and as the spirited horse started off my little four-year-old legs went flying. When the horse began to go too fast, I let go. But I had held on too long. I fell flat on my head on a tin can in the road and the blow and the cut on my nose made me cross-eyed. This was real punishment and quite enough for a young girl who had disobeyed her parents. It was a year before I had an operation to straighten that eye. There is a scar on my nose now that reminds me of that flying run behind that horse and buggy! In a round-about-way it also made me hate bananas.

After the operation on my eye, I was often taken to Los Angeles for follow up visits. Once Bessie left me behind with a bag of bananas she intended for our entire family, while she visited the Normal School (teacher's college). I don't remember how long she was gone but I do remember there were very few bananas left when she got back. After that I could not even bear the smell of bananas and even today will avoid eating them at all costs! Maybe I was also a bit clumsy. Once I went to a party to keep Josie company. We walked the half mile to the Willows Station and from there took the local electric car, intending to get off at Fourth Street. As the car slowed down for the Fourth Street stop the motorman cut the power and we were silently gliding along the middle of the block when I decided we had stopped. It was a moonless night, and I blithely hopped down the steps to get off. We hadn't stopped and I fell flat on my face. Fortunately, Josie and the conductor came as fast as they could after the car was brought to a sudden stop and they picked me up. I said I was alright, and told Josie we should go to the party. Once there we didn't stay long. I was in worse shape than I had admitted to.

I may have been accident prone, but I also had Grandpa Moore, the only grandpa I ever knew, who always showed concern and interest over my latest scrapes and bruises. My parents used to talk about how he suffered from severe pain and seizures, but Grandpa Moore never complained, he was always cheerful and happy to see me. He lived across Atlantic Avenue from us with his wife Margaret and three children, all a good deal older than me, on his twenty-acre orange ranch in a large three-story home. His attic was one of my favorite places. From there one could see for miles. When the mist of the early morning cleared, I could see Catalina and the mountains to the north.

My greatest delight was to run up hill to this big home when I thought Grandpa Moore would be collecting eggs. I can hear him now calling his great flock of hens to feed them. I can smell the hay in the goat barn where the two of us wandered from nest to nest gathering lovely brown eggs. There was always one white "China egg" in each nest. I supposed the hens wouldn't know where to lay their eggs if it wasn't for this fake one. Well, there were usually eight or ten real eggs beside it. Finding each nest was the joy of my early life.

I remember the dogs and cats at this big home. Carlo, the big shaggy St. Bernard and little "Pug" the pug dog. There were three or four cats and usually some kittens. There was a special dish for each of the dogs and cats and like a drill team, each moved on to inspect each other's supper, not realizing they were getting the same meal. It was always the same parade and exchange. Don't ask me why, except they may have suspected their own wasn't quite as good or as much as the next.

Getting Around

Growing up we traveled to places by train, the Pacific Electric railroad and good old Tommy pulling our wagon or buggy. But there were also bicycles.

Cycling became popular in Long Beach in the late 1890s when I was about 8-years-old. A popular bicycle was one that had a very large front wheel and a little one trailing along behind. It was called a Penny Farthing since the side view resembled a larger British penny leading a smaller farthing. My brother Tom found a worn out one left behind somewhere and brought it home as a curiosity and tried to repair it. I think he may have ridden it once or twice but soon lost interest and relegated it to our barn. The rest of us hadn't lost interest. I remember Helen and Norah would laboriously wheel it to the top of the rise on Atlantic and Willow Street and coast, one on the seat of the wheel and the other running beside to be sure it did not tip over. Down they would go to our driveway where they turned in and fell onto the lawn or sand by the side of the road.

As time went on, we acquired "regular" bicycles, nice, modern at that time, two wheeled ones. My sister Bessie rode hers to her teaching assignment at the high school. She paid one of us to dust and polish it every evening and that bicycle became a show piece. Being cared for so lovingly, it outlasted many of those the rest of us had.

My younger sister, Kathleen, even at the age of eleven was a fearless cyclist. Her intrepid spirit led her to adventures I never would have dared. However, one Saturday morning in 1905 she met her Waterloo.

After finishing her music lesson, she left the Meserve home at the top of Cherry Avenue, in an adventurous mood. Travelling back home on her bicycle, she decided it would be fun to coast down the hill. She started out without a care, putting her feet on the handle bars. She rapidly gained speed and was practically flying down Cherry, the pedals whirling so fast she couldn't begin to get her feet on them to decrease her speed. She tried once and nearly crashed. She knew the only way to keep body and soul together was by again placing her feet on the handle bars.

A man driving a gravel wagon up the hill on Cherry to the gravel pit yelled something at her but she was so frightened she didn't hear a word. If he told her she was risking her life it was no news to her. She wasn't doing it willingly. She had long since lost all enthusiasm for this wild ride. She was quite sure the only end would be drowning in the ocean as she shot off the bluff at the end of Cherry Avenue into the breakers of the Pacific. Even that might be easier than crashing into a tree!

Faster and faster she flew. Four boys at the side of the road stood up from folding newspapers for delivery to wave their caps in a wild "hurrah" watching this brave girl do what they never had the courage to do. Little did they know how Kathleen's heart raced with the bicycle wheels. Her brain whirled. Where would she end it all? Who would find her remains and break the news to Mother and Father? What would her fine bicycle look like wrapped around her neck?

It seemed like hours, but it was only seven tortuous minutes until the ride came to an end. It was something she would never forget. Where others might have swooned into unconsciousness, Kathleen stuck to her bike, feet upon the handle bars hands holding the front wheel straight for dear life. She knew if once that wheel veered one fraction of an inch she was lost. She had sense enough to realize that somewhere her speed might decrease and perhaps if she kept upright long enough she might slow down before she crashed into the ocean, or worse, hit some horse and buggy slowly crossing Cherry at Tenth, State (Pacific Coast Highway today), or Anaheim Street.

As she approached State Street, she saw what might be her salvation. Somehow swirling waters of a February downpour had washed a sandy strip along the side of Cherry Avenue. She had sailed into sandy places before on her bicycle. In fact, she had learned to ride a bike that way, as we all had. It was lessons learned on how to stop when riding Tom's solid rubber-tired high wheeled, pedal-less Penny Farthing. This early training was what saved Kathleen, for she knew just how to sail into this sandy strip and let the bike go one way and she the other. She was a shaky and wiser girl after she shook off the sand and headed home, walking slowly as she tried to catch her breath and balance. She took the long way around Signal Hill and no one commented on her flushed face so it was some months before she brought herself to tell us all of her near-death encounter that Saturday after her music lesson.

Automobiles arrived and bicycles went out of favor, along with the horse and buggy. Fred Bixby of the Rancho Los Alamitos was arguably the first to own an automobile in the area, driving it into town for the Pacific Electric rail opening on July 4, 1902. It was a "White Steamer" and created quite a stir, and soon everyone wanted one! By 1904 the city had set a speed limit of eight miles per hour for both bicycles and automobiles, for the safety of pedestrians.

I was very young when our neighbor got a little old Oldsmobile. She was used to her horse bolting and running away when the horse heard the whistle of the train coming along California Avenue. Old habits die hard and our neighbor would clutch the steering wheel and called out "Ho Dandy! Ho Dandy!" whenever she heard the train approaching. That's the way we all felt when we turned our horses out to pasture and let ourselves in for the hazards of driving automobiles.

Automobiles took off like wildfire. In 1905 there were 75 in Long Beach, ten years later 1800, including one owned by my brother Tom. Then the jitney idea took hold.

Tom's friend A.H. Kirkendall came to Long Beach from Phoenix, Arizona, in March 1914 with a novel idea — using automobiles to transport passengers. The idea had originated three years earlier to handle traffic in the Arizona capital which didn't have a massive street car system like Los Angeles. Here the pay-to-ride motor car was a boon to the residents of the newly opened housing tracts out from Phoenix. Long Beach, however, had the highly efficient Pacific Electric rail line, but Kirkendall decided to give the Arizona idea a go.

He began his Long Beach operation using his Ford to carry people from Ocean and Pine along East Fourth Street. Within two weeks other auto owners quickly adopted the idea of using their own vehicles to make money.

My sister Bessie, the town historian, told me it was Long Beach's John H. Meteer who coined the name "jitney" from the one-time colloquial term for a 5-cent piece. Since the cost of carrying passengers in these auto busses was 5-cents, the term stuck. I later read that by December 1914, there were more than 1000 cars-for-hire operating in Los Angeles alone. Independent jitney drivers' competition became so great that Long Beach was forced to adopt regulations that prevented them from racing against each other to get a prospective passenger waiting at a corner. In addition, the ordinance limited the number of passengers the jitneys could carry and prevented riders from standing on the running boards. It also required that each jitney bus owner take out $10,000 ($280,000 in 2021) indemnity insurance.

By 1916 there were 131 independent jitneys cruising various streets in Long Beach and the Pacific Electric Company began feeling the jitney competition. Those living in outlying areas of Long Beach began to fear that because of the decrease in PE usage the electric railroad would abandon certain of its lines. The city decided the solution to this problem was to franchise jitney operations. In November 1916 Ray Julian, Charles Bean and others bought, on a bid of $6500 ($166,000 in 2021), a ten-year franchise for exclusive auto bus rights on Atlantic Avenue and Fourth Street. The franchise required the newly formed Long Beach Transportation Company to pay 3 per cent of the gross receipts annually to the city. Gradually busses and cars took over from the railroad and Pacific Electric, but I still look back fondly on the "good old" horse and buggy days.

HOLIDAYS

Fourth of July

The Fourth of July signaled the official opening of the tourist season in Long Beach. It came to mean a picnic on the beach, with lots going on. Father drove the big wagon in order to take the whole family. We parked it on the sand dunes where the wild verbena and other flowers grew. There was a bathhouse where my older siblings rented bathing suits and paid to use the bathhouse.

The big breakers were considered too rough for us younger ones. We were content to tuck up our skirts and play in the wet sand. We wandered along, wading in the tide, picking up sea shells and sand dollars, and digging for the plentiful small clams that made a delicious soup after we reached home.

Often the celebration began early, such as in 1896 when I was five. Though I don't remember it too well, my historian sister Bessie told me it was "historic" because it was the year of the city's first beauty contest. On July 2, 500 people congregated in the Tabernacle to witness the "Carnival of Trades," in which thirty young women, dressed in costumes signifying the business they represented, marched around the stage saluting pageant winner, Miss Johnson, Queen of Trade.

The highlight of the program was Mrs. Tutt, the manager of the Electric Light Company, who appeared in a robe studded with incandescent lights, holding a staff which supported a small arc lamp. None of my sisters participated. They laughed saying what were they to dress up as? A pigeon or chicken?

Thousands of people came to town for that holiday in 1896, enjoying the surf, yacht races, and diving exhibitions at the end of the pier. In the evening everyone was treated to a mock naval battle between two ships, the *Point Loma* and the *Santa Barbara,* who bombarded each other with rockets and Roman candles. That event I remember!

The 4th of July meant noise, and plenty of it. The band played part of the time and then there were speeches, which we children ignored. We lit fire crackers, which frightened small babies like my brother Frank. At last, tired, sunburned and still happy we piled into the wagon and went home.

Until Frank got older, we rarely stayed for the evening fireworks on the beach, but we could watch it from our house if we were not too sleepy by that time. That evening my older siblings lit any fire crackers they had left, gathering any leftovers the next day to continue the celebration a little longer, much to the dismay of Mother who tried to keep Frank from crying!

Halloween

We all looked forward to holidays. Halloween was a time when more "tricks" were played than "treats" handed out. One Halloween we were all told we could not go out with some of our friends that evening. Mother had heard some older boys planned to join our group and show us what Halloween really could be. She knew that meant mischief!

We were a disgruntled lot, but couldn't disobey our parents. So, we remained at home and pacified ourselves by making taffy. Seeing our sour faces Mother allowed us to stay up later than usual, but Bessie, who had to teach the next day, went to bed at her usual time.

Three or four boys, upset by our refusal to join them in their Halloween pranks, decided to play one on us. Thinking we were already in bed, they began to brush the outdoor sleeping porch with tree branches. Bessie, who suffered from nightmares and the only one asleep, woke up screaming. Bessie's screams terrified the boys who dropped their branches, frightened out of their wits, and ran, thinking they may have called forth a banshee!

Christmas

Christmas in our large family was something very special. We didn't need expensive gifts to warm our young hearts, just the fragrance of fruitcakes baking and the tradition of making an English plum pudding was enough.

One year while Mother was spending the day in Los Angeles buying Christmas gifts, Jack and Ethel decided to surprise her by having the plum pudding all made and boiled by the time the train brought her home.

Many little fingers helped with seeding raisins. Many little feet ran errands to help Jack and Ethel. In creating the Christmas plum pudding, we always added a ring, a dime and a thimble to the batter. The batter was tied up in a large white cloth and boiled in an enormous copper boiler, hung from a copper stick laid across the top of the boiler. I don't know how long it took a fifteen-pound plum pudding to cook. I only know it smelled wonderful, and to us little ones it seemed a very long time before it was done.

We met Mother at the train at Burnett Street and California Avenue and no one gave away the secret, but I think she must have guessed the moment she got in the house. There is only one thing that smells like a plum pudding and that's a plum pudding!

The time came to take it out of the huge copper boiler. Jack was tall and strong and he stood on a chair to have a better lift for it. Young and old stood around the big kitchen, holding their breath. Up it came and Jack gave an awful groan. He and Ethel had forgotten to put a plate under it. The bottom had burned out of the cloth and the pudding was disintegrating into the water.

Mother tried to cheer them up with, "Get the thimble, the dime and the ring and we'll all help with making another pudding tomorrow." We never forgot the tragedy of the Christmas pudding that was to have been such a surprise for Mother. Well, in hindsight, I guess you could say she was surprised!

When I was about eight years old the Christmas season found us pinched for funds. The family talked it all over and decided we could forgo individual gifts this particular Christmas. The family needed a new stove and thought a new kitchen range would be a big gift for all. When we younger ones were presented with the idea, we agreed, but that had been weeks before Christmas. We were a bit grim about our earlier family agreement and tried to keep our chins up as the 25th of December approached.

That Christmas Eve we were kept busy making candy and cakes. True, the new stove was doing its part in helping create rich delicious odors which numbed our senses. But this day lacked the sparkle and excitement of last-minute shopping, and looking through key holes to try to see packages being wrapped in rooms where we were unceremoniously told not to enter. There was no Christmas tree, since there were no presents to place underneath.

We sang carols and went to bed quietly. That morning we were suddenly awakened at 4:25 a.m. by an earthquake! It was heavy enough to shake down pans and other items. Father discouraged the belief in Santa Claus bringing presents, but the thought did cross our young minds that perhaps Father was wrong and Santa's sled had landed on our roof. Only later did we find it was an earthquake centered in Riverside County near Hemet.

When things settled down our stout young hearts struggled to be merry but it took a lot of lifting of bootstraps to pull up our spirits. We went into the kitchen to look at our fine new range where bacon was frying and eggs were being scrambled. Then Mother told us that Bessie wanted to see us in her study. This was unusual. If Bessie was in her study, she was sure to be busy. As we knocked on Bessie's study door, she opened it with a "Merry Christmas to everyone," and flung the door wide open.

There on the table were beautifully wrapped small packages, with our names on them. Everyone squealed with delight. I could hardly wait to open mine. Inside was a harmonica. Even a more expensive gift couldn't have brought me more of a thrill. Anne's was a game of cards called "Authors." Caroline's was a new red hair ribbon.

Bessie hadn't been able to envision us without some gift, tiny though it might be. All of the presents cost very little, yet I am sure none of us in any of our Christmases together ever had such a memorable one. I don't believe there ever was a happier group in all the years of our family Christmases than that year when Bessie became our Santa Claus.

There were other Christmases when the older ones were teaching school. The family was divided into two groups. The "Millionaire Bunch" as Kathleen and I called them and the "Penniless Bunch" which was comprised of Anne, Kathleen, Frank and me. The Penniless Bunch, as the name implies had little but initiative and willing hands, to make a contribution toward Christmas gifts under the Christmas tree.

We put a lot of effort into making our home-made gifts. One year Kathleen borrowed Anne's wood burning set and etched Anne's name on a napkin ring she carved out of a piece of orange wood. Anne drew a cardboard man in overalls with patches on his pants. The patches were of sandpaper. The printing was "Scratch Your Matches on my Patches." It was a gift for Tom, from us all, and years after coal oil lamps were replaced by electricity Tom cherished that gift. No one could prevail upon him to remove it from his bedroom wall. Anne's napkin ring is still in a drawer. No one seems to be able to toss it out. How we cling to the reminders of our wonderful days when we four were "The Penniless Bunch."

There were clear cold Christmas Eves when the stars shone brightly. No smog, and no street lights. Mother bundled us up for the horse and buggy ride into town for our church Christmas tree decorating. We jogged along singing Christmas carols and looked for candle lit Christmas trees strung with popcorn and cranberries. There were only a few homes along Atlantic Avenue then but each lighted tree we passed brought on oohs and aahs and shouts of joy. What fun! Maybe we missed the snow and sleigh rides of children in the east but no one ever had more joy on Christmas Eve than we did on that three-mile ride to church to recite poems and receive a stocking filled with candy.

Tom used to hold an annual Christmas party during Christmas week. He started the tradition when we were still at our ranch but later moved it to our Sunrise Boulevard home. All his employees, which numbered from around eighteen in his early years in the business to thirty-four in later years, were invited. When we had the ranch, we served our specialty — squab — later switching to turkey.

We spent hours decorating the house and preparing dinner. One Christmas we made tiny place holders out of grain sacks at which three small mice nibbled! Following the meal, which usually consisted of five courses, we would all socialize with speeches, music, games, ending with Christmas bonus checks being passed out. This "business-family" Christmas event was a wonderful tradition that everyone looked forward to.

We also celebrated the twelfth day of Christmas, which was an old English tradition. On January 12th it was the custom to burn all the Christmas decorations, each one of us taking a handful and making a wish for the coming year.

I remember one January, I believe it was 1910, when the Signal Hill Tennis Club held a party. The celebration took place on the 21st, so we didn't have decorations to burn. Invitations were issued in rhyme on burned paper with a gold seal. Each guest was told to come masked. Josie impersonated a gypsy fortune teller. I dressed as the Queen of Clubs, Helen the Queen of Hearts, Norah as an Irish maid, Anne as a colonial maid. Helen won the backward spelling bee in which the words were recited backwards and players had to figure out, and spell, the word correctly. It was loads of fun!

Empire Day

One tradition we were sad to leave behind was the celebration commemorating Queen Victoria's May 24th birthday. My older siblings still remembered parades, singing patriotic songs, and waving the Union Jack. When the Queen died in 1901 her subjects still wanted to honor her accomplishments so Parliament issued a proclamation establishing May 24th as Empire Day. Our family and other former British subjects now living in southern California decided to celebrate "Empire Day," after all if the Irish had their St. Patrick's Day festivities, and the Italians Columbus Day, why not a holiday for British Americans?

In 1913, 20,000 former British subjects living in southern California came together in Long Beach for the region's first Empire Day celebration. The *Daily Telegram* of May 23, 1913, described the next day's event:

The greatest British celebration ever held on foreign soil. That is what the committee in charge of the arrangements for the big Empire Day celebration to be held in this city tomorrow expects the fete to be. From all over the southland will come those who formerly lived under the British flag. Drawing card features of the day will be the presence of the British man-of-war, Shearwater, 60 of whose sailors will act as an escort for the veterans in the parade; there will be a big program of athletic stunts, national games, the parade, music and the natural attractions of Long Beach. The parade will be elaborate, with several floats each representing dominions or possessions of the English nation, the participants of each float being natives of the that particular country represented. The parade will reach the auditorium where speeches will be made. Five hundred dollars' worth of prizes will be given to the winners of the various contests.

Of course, our family participated. Earlier in the week Bessie presented a paper on the celebration to the Civic League of Signal Hill.

However, what was to have been a day of joy turned into one of tragedy when a rotten girder outside the entrance of the municipal auditorium gave way. Thirty-eight people died and approximately 200 were injured. Fortunately, all members of the Harnett family escaped injury. Days later Bessie and others from Poly High School arranged for flowers to be delivered to local victims and those injured. Flags were flown at half-mast for the remainder of the school year.

Long Beach felt responsible for the tragedy. Doctors donated their services free of charge. Ten thousand dollars was quickly raised to aid the victims. Later, attorneys advised the City that they were not financially responsible for the disaster, but Long Beach citizens believed they had a moral responsibility for the tragedy and overwhelmingly voted to add a special tax levy of 20 cents to each $100 of their assessed property valuation to take care of the sick, helpless and dependent victims of the disaster.

Celebrating Empire Day continued in southern California, with Santa Monica hosting the event in 1914. Though long considered one of the worst disasters in California history, and one Long Beach would rather forget, my brother Tom helped plan another Empire Day celebration in 1921. Several local English societies including the Sons and Daughters of St. George, the Thistle Club, the Heather Club and Daughters of the Empire, aided in the planning the event. No marching bands or floats, just speeches, music and greeting old friends at St. Luke's Hall.

Fourth of July 1902.
Courtesy of the Long Beach History Collection, Long Beach Public Library

The Long Beach Milling Company was always ready for any holiday.
Courtesy of the Long Beach History Collection, Long Beach Public Library

Mother

My Mother was beautiful. She was born in November 1848, in a great four-story stone house which stood with its back to Bedlam Insane Asylum (also known as Bethlem Hospital) along Lambeth Road in London. She was one of twelve children born to Irish surgeon Peter Berrell and his English wife Eloza Hutchinson.

The origin of the hospital went back to the 13th century and became known for cruelty and inhumane treatment. When a group of Members of Parliament visited the hospital in 1814, they were shocked at the small cells where people were chained to the beds or walls. Just one blanket was provided to each patient to protect them from rats and cold. In 1815, the hospital was moved to the site Mother knew, at St George's Fields, just south of the Thames.

Several lessons had already been learned, and the introduction of new staff in a new building brought reforms. The patients were now kept clean, well clothed, and were not under any restraint. It was at this new "modern" Bedlam where Dr. Berrell, Mother's father, was a Governor, and often worked.

In 1838, when the grounds of Bethlem Hospital were enlarged, a triangle of vacant land was left and assigned to Governors of the hospital to build homes, including Grandfather Berrell. With nothing but a high wall between the Berrells and the mentally ill of Bedlam, Mother's family sometimes saw a face appear over the wall staring at them as the Berrell family enjoyed the sunny back garden.

My grandfather and many other physicians and surgeons went to parties at Bedlam where the sane and insane mixed. Guests paid money for such an experience, which helped support the hospital. Mother told how sometimes the quite sane were mistaken for the insane. One guest was seen gathering up the teaspoons and an inquiring doctor was told, "Oh, never mind, she's a kleptomaniac and someone will get the silver teaspoons from under her bed when the party is over."

In 1933, my sister Kathleen and I visited England and looked for the Bethlem Hospital Mother knew from childhood. We found it had been moved to the suburbs of Croydon three years earlier and the old building torn down. The Bishop's Place and Lambeth Palace alone remained of the familiar environs of Mother's girlhood. There she was baptized and married to rear her own brood of fourteen.

Since grandfather Berrell was a member of the Dramatic, Equestrian, and Musical Sick Fund, which included author Charles Dickens, there was always a box at the theater for his family. Many times, Mother would tell us of seeing David Garrick, Sir Henry Irving, Ellen Terry and many other famous actors and actresses of that day.

Today children play at imitating Superman or some other hero. For us, Mother's tales of the theater encouraged us to emulate the great performers she had seen in her youth. Frequently we had "Shakespeare Night" when we congregated under the old pepper tree on our farm and took on the role of actors and actresses. On moonlight nights we gathered in the hay fields which were interspersed with haycocks that gave us a mound to stand on and spout poetry or preach a sermon from the Bible.

Four of Mother's uncles were surgeons of the Royal College of Surgeons and Mother also had a flare for surgery. Of all his children it was Mother that grandfather called when he needed an assistant. This served her well taking care of all the mishaps that befell her children.

Black hair, very blue eyes, a lovely English complexion, never over exposed to our California sun as those of her children were with their outdoor activities. How she tried to get her daughters to wear sun bonnets. She said afterwards that our ranch must be sown with them for they seldom came back to the house.

Mother was a religious woman, a life-long member of the Episcopal church. She was instrumental in founding the first Episcopal church in Long Beach which held services in Pickles' Hall on First Street.

My recollections of Pickles' Hall are few. I do remember, however, that the windows were soaped to take the place of shades. I also can't forget that I dearly loved the 11 a.m. Sunday morning service when Holmes Mawser was there with his mother. He always misbehaved, and was taken out and spanked soundly in the Sunday School room. He was a pincher and a hitter and I disliked him immensely. I have to admit the sounds of his spanking and loud crying, were joy to my ears. Not very Christian of me!

Mother and my sister Ethel played the organ for the choir. When Ethel was organist, Mother sang in the choir with Bessie. Mother later helped raise funds for a formal church building which became St. Luke's Episcopal Church.

St. Luke's, at Fifth and Locust, was dedicated in August 1900. My brother Jack helped with construction and in wiring the lights. Reverend W. E. Jacob was at the dedication and remained minister there until 1902. He had taken charge of the Episcopal mission in Long Beach in 1897, riding on horseback between San Pedro, Wilmington and the village of Long Beach. I do remember we had Sunday School picnics at Reverend Jacob's home on Terminal Island. We had such a wonderful day — wading in the ocean, bathing and playing games on the sand and of course a tasty picnic lunch. Perhaps best of all was that we got to ride a train to Terminal Island.

Reverend Jacob was replaced with a minister from Philadelphia, Reverend Charles Murphy. We always laugh when we recall how Reverend Murphy wrote asking what kind of Native American dialect we spoke here!

In 1917 a lot at 7th and Atlantic was purchased and a larger church built. It had to be torn down after the 1933 Long Beach earthquake, and a year later a new sanctuary was dedicated. Tom was responsible for much of the growth of the church. He was a senior warden for more than 50 years, seeing St. Luke's transform from a mission to one with a large congregation.

Yes, Mother was lovely. A small woman but very active and capable. Her beauty impressed me as child. I remember sitting beside her in church one day. A few rows in front of us another child sat beside her mother, a woman with a leathery California complexion and not too well dressed and wondering if her daughter thought her as beautiful as I thought my mother.

Beauty was not all. We knew we could take any problem to Mother and she would always listen and advise. Yet with all our love, childlike, we never thought to offer her further help once our chores were done. One day she was peeling potatoes at the sink and I noticed tears on her cheeks. Although I had already finished my allotted chores for the day, I took the paring knife from her and finished peeling the potatoes. After witnessing a tearful Mother, I was more than willing to help where and when I could, anything to prevent seeing her cry. Why the tears? I never knew but years afterwards decided it must have been that she had discovered she was to add another child to the already large family which included: Jane Elizabeth (Bessie) born January 17, 1873; Ernest Thomas (Tom) October 9, 1874; John Abraham (Jack) July 9, 1877; Margaret Ethel

(Ethel) April 14, 1879; Geoffrey Berrell May 30, 1881; Josephine (Josie) April 9, 1883; Helen Mary (Helen) August 9, 1884; Norah Berrell (Norah) November 8, 1885; Anne Hutchinson (Nannie) February 16, 1887; Edward Hutchinson February 23, 1888; Julia Caroline (Caroline), 1889.

I (Ivy) was the first of three children born in Long Beach, entering the family January 26, 1891; Kathleen (Katie) arrived December 5, 1895; Francis Berrell (Frank) June 26, 1897.

Father was often questioned when shopping in the little village of Long Beach about the many youngsters in the wagon. He replied, "Yes, all of these are my children, but these are not ALL of my children."

Father

Father, Ernest Harnett, was born October 7, 1840, at Wormdale Farm, Newington, Kent, England, the youngest child of Thomas Harnett and Anne Dodd. His family wasn't as large as Mother's; there were just five children — Father (Ernest), Alfred and Frank, and sisters Julia and Selina (aka Sarah). His side of the family can be traced back through the family estate, Thrognall, to around 1804, when Thrognall was sold by the family who had owned it for nearly 200 years, the owner wanting to retire to London. The *London Morning Post*, July 20, 1804, described it as having "an excellent brick stucco house, with double coach house, stabling for four horses, four barns, a greenhouse, numerous out buildings, large gardens planted with fruit trees, 190 acres of choice land with luxuriant views over green fields, refreshed with beautiful sea views, protected from the wind by lofty trees and shrubberies." I remember seeing the date 1605, over the fireplace when Kathleen and I visited in 1933. Even then my sister and I could see the "fake" windows on the manor. It seemed that when King William III imposed a "window tax" in 1696, every other window upstairs was kicked out, but to all outward appearances looked like windows — with curtains and shades painted on them.

I'm not sure of much of our family history before then. The Harnetts may go back even further since Newington (meaning New Town), the closest town, was built on a Roman settlement dating to 30 B.C.

It was wonderful when Kathleen and I were able to travel to the places we had heard so much about growing up. Being born in America, we relished visiting the country of our siblings' birth. Father had a picture of Wormdale, where the family lived. It was only a quarter mile from Thrognall. When we visited in July 1933, we looked for the little trees seen in the picture which our Grandmother Harnett had planted in the front garden. Now, in 1933, they were huge chestnut trees. We also visited Chesley, another family home across the lane from Thrognall. Here Father's nephew, Arthur, who married his cousin Catherine Mary Harnett, the daughter of his brother Frank, lived for years.

As I mentioned before, Father loved mathematics. After a few hours of work on our farm, he would come in, find a large sheet of paper, perhaps one in which the laundry had been wrapped, take out a small stub of a pencil and work for what seemed like hours on some mathematical problem. Sometimes he talked about algebraic equations with mathematics teachers from the high school, but he seemed to have a better understanding of arithmetic than the instructors!

When not figuring out some scientific formula, and farming, he assisted my brother Tom at the Long Beach Milling Company. He was there when Tom took over the company in 1897 but retired from the business in 1905 at the age of 65. Besides having a love of equations, he was very fond of machinery. I remember him building himself a lathe and various other gadgets.

One story handed down in the family was that Father always wore a full beard but decided to shave for his wedding day. He contracted pneumonia and nearly died. He never shaved again, though he did trim his beard himself and allowed Mother to trim his hair. Dress meant very little to him and I remember the trouble Mother had getting him properly attired for church. Weddings in the family were even more troublesome for her. Why should he wear a tie? His beard would cover it. But he was devoted to Mother and she had her way.

He was definitely a very godly man. Many a cold winter morning I can remember seeing him beside the fire with his Bible on his knees and Dummelow's Concordance beside him. He was a great man for attending church. He would walk down to the early services at St. Luke's Episcopal Church, then attend Reverend Taubman's Men's Bible Class, and finish the morning by going back to St. Luke's for the eleven o-clock service. In the evening he would often go to services at the Baptist Church.

He was 51 when I was born. I can't remember his hair being anything but white, but I do remember his English accent was hard for some of our younger southern California neighbors to understand. He was a strict father, but a loving one and he had the love and respect of his family. Sadly, he died February 20th, 1918, after being hit by a car on Atlantic near Burnett Street in Long Beach. A few weeks before his accidental death at age 77 he demonstrated to Dr. Harvey that he could still jump straight up and tap his boots together before he hit the floor again. The young doctor said he himself could not even do that!

It was a hit and run accident that killed Father when he was walking to his mid-week prayer meeting at a nearby church. He was struck by an automobile driven by a 15-year-old boy, who had taken the family car for what some later said was an errand, others a joy ride. It was believed, though never proven, that death was instantaneous. A sharpened piece of one of the headlights jabbed into Father's head. His right leg was fractured below the knee and his nose was crushed.

The boy, Elmer Joselyn, fled the scene. Arriving home upset, his mother finally got him to tell what happened. She and a lawyer later took him to the police station to report the accident. Elmer was unable to give an intelligible account, not even remembering where the accident occurred or what direction he was going when it happened. It was pitch-dark, it was raining, there were no sidewalks in the area and all he could remember was that as he moved along in the storm, at ordinary speed, he saw a dark figure in the street ahead, tried to dodge, felt the impact and then lost all sense of his surroundings, but somehow proceeded home to tell the story to his mother.

We did not press charges, since no amount of legal action could bring back Father. Following Father's death, the remaining family moved Mother from the farm house at 2481 Atlantic to a two-story house built for her at 730 Sunrise Boulevard, in Long Beach. Her health began to fail in 1926, and despite doctors and family efforts to prolong her live, Mother joined Father in death on September 13, 1928. Tom and I continued living in the Sunrise home until 1945, when we moved to smaller quarters. However, the house stayed in the family, with my brother Frank buying the property.

Father's funeral was held February 23, 1918, four days after the funeral of his daughter Bessie. One friend remembered meeting Father downtown after Bessie's death and telling him "I don't know why I couldn't have been the one to go instead of her." Some later said she died of complications from the influenza epidemic of 1918-1919. But that is not true since the epidemic is said to have started in the fall of 1918 and no one else in the family came down with the disease following Bessie's passing. However, Josie fell victim in December 1918. Fortunately, Josie survived. Pneumonia was the cause listed on Bessie's death certificate, a condition she tried to fight off for three long weeks. We were all devastated by her death.

Geoffrey and Caroline

The first break in our family circle was Geoffrey. I never knew my little brother. He was spoken of often. Mother always said he was the most beautiful of all her children — golden curls and blue eyes and an adorable way of saying "Mothurr." He used to look over the stairs from the nursery and call down to her, "Is dinner ready, Mothurr," in a quaint drawl. But his young life was taken from their midst in 1884, at the age of two, leaving behind four siblings.

His death was the result of a faulty drain. No one knew the repairman left a germ ridden tile out after he completed his work until Bessie went to the hospital with scarlet fever. Soon after little Geoffrey came down with diphtheritic croup, an infection of the upper airway, which obstructs breathing and causes a characteristic barking cough. Bessie recovered to come home to a home empty of her beloved baby brother.

In 1907 poor Bessie had far reaching complications from the mumps that affected the family that year. She was advised to take a year's leave of absence from her post as head of the History Department at Long Beach High School. After months of recuperation at home, she set sail for England, sufficiently recovered. She came home to a house empty of a sister.

It happened on May 23, 1907. Caroline and I were planning an early game of tennis, and since Father was away, Caroline had taken over his usual chore of starting the morning wood and coal fire in the stove. Father always laid the fire and then poured a little coal oil over it to insure it started well. I can see him now — pouring it from a little sardine can of kerosene, which is what Caroline did that fateful morning. There wasn't much oil in the can and the can filled with gas. It exploded, bursting into flames, which quickly leapt to Caroline's light gown. I can still hear Caroline's screams of "Mother, Mother," as she ran to Mother's bed, a living torch, and seeing Mother throw a quilt around her.

Edward put out the flames spreading on the kitchen wall so quickly the wood scarcely burned. Mother was not injured but both of Josie's hands were badly burned. When the doctor arrived he said Mother, who poured olive oil all over Caroline, would be responsible for saving her life if Caroline lived. For twelve agonizing hours we stayed by her bed. But as the day drew to a close, she slipped away. We loved her and she was gone. We comforted each other but no one ever took her place. No one could. And we had to tell Father and Bessie.

Father was on a mining trip to the mountains near Escondido, but rushed home when word finally reached him. Bessie was away in England and didn't hear the news for some time. She was beside herself that she missed her 17-year-old sister's funeral.

Eight young women dressed in white, classmates of Caroline's were pallbearers at her funeral.

Bessie

Bessie was like a second mother to all of us. The oldest of the brood, she set an example that was hard to follow. She had recently graduated from Rochester College and had already passed both junior and senior Oxford examinations before the family left Kent. She was able to easily pass the California teacher's certification test. In 1906 she was asked to spend her summer vacation teaching history at the University of California, Berkeley. It became part of her regular summer routine, teaching at the University while taking classes which earned her a Master's degree in Education. Josie also spent several summers at the University, along with Bessie, and following Bessie's death she took over her sister's teaching duties at the high school.

Shortly after we arrived in Long Beach in 1890, Judge Henry Clay Dillon, who had a large home and a farm on Signal Hill, asked Bessie to move in with the family and teach his six youngsters. There were five girls and one boy. Florence was the oldest at 12, twins Fannie and Anna 9, Josephine 6, James 4 and Viva only a year old. Bessie was just 17, but with her extended schooling in England she was well prepared. She taught in an upstairs room of their house which was furnished with blackboards, tables, chairs, and even a dunce stool! Josephine Dillon once remarked that Bessie had been brought in to tame them! Later Judge Dillon recommended Bessie for a teaching position at the city's first high school built in 1895. Bessie taught in the history department and it wasn't long until she was its head.

The Dillon's settled on Signal Hill in 1887, purchasing 160 acres. By 1892 Judge Dillon had divided his land into 20 acre lots but kept 40 acres on which to live. Bessie must have been a positive influence in the lives of the Dillon children, besides teaching them the "basics" she instilled in them a love of music and theater. Florence and Viva Dillon became opera singers, Fannie a composer and Josephine went on to become an actress, and the first Mrs. Clark Gable.

Bessie also educated us without us realizing it because she made learning such fun. I loved the enormous old pepper tree with its big limbs which I would nestle into reading my favorite book. Knowing what I liked Bessie borrowed books from the school and library which instilled in me a lifetime love of reading.

Bessie was full of knowledge, which she shared with her students. In 1914 she made an interesting discovery while on a school outing at the Rancho Los Alamitos — the site of an ancient Native American settlement. Some of the boys, who hunted ducks out that way, had heard Japanese vegetable growers, who leased land from Fred Bixby, talk about finding Indian pestles and mortars further down toward the bay. When the boys told this to Bessie, she arranged another field trip to gather artifacts for the school's May 1915 Long Beach Pageant. While no relics of great value were found, the ground having been thoroughly searched by others, the students picked up some shell objects and were convinced they had stumbled upon an old village.

Then came the Pageant. This was put on by the pupils of Polytechnic High School and presented the history of Long Beach beginning with its Native American roots. Bessie had students write scripts using material she had researched and organized. The army of student actors represented Spanish soldiers, sailors, friars and caballeros from the days of Cabrillo and later periods before the Gold Rush. Mingled with these characterizations of the people of the past were more recent scenes such as the sale of the first lot in Long Beach. Real sheep were used in the sheep shearing episode about the Bixby ranch and the pageant closed with a symbolic representation of the progress of Long Beach with waves of the sea.

The Pageant was a tremendous undertaking for a high school and could not have been handled without the assistance of the city and the work of my sister Bessie. It was a huge four-night presentation performed under the trees at Bixby Park, by 1,200 Poly High School students. The performances were seen and praised by more than 9,000 persons. Who in Long Beach would want to miss it?

Bessie died on February 16, 1918. She was only forty-five years-old. Years afterwards she was still spoken of with love and affection by not only her family, but the community. The entire student body of the high school attended her memorial service at St. Luke's Episcopal Church. Following the service, the students formed an avenue from the church down Linden, through which the casket was borne, with our family following behind. At Sunnyside Cemetery a student honor guard escorted her casket from the gate to her grave site.

There were many tributes to Bessie. Reverend Booth stated how she was the unacknowledged force behind revising Long Beach's charter, with city fathers turning to her for clarification and guidelines. Professor Burcham told how she helped organize the first student body and instituted the first self-governing student system in southern California, a model later copied by other schools. She also established a loan scholarship fund at Poly, open to students who could not afford to continue their education.

The research she had done for the 1915 Pageant was the start of her contribution to a statewide history project called the "California Local History Annals" led by Luther Ingersoll. She wrote in the morning, getting up about 4 a.m., put on a comforter and sat and wrote her history. But death took her before she could finish. Ingersoll asked Kathleen to finish Bessie's "Annals of the City of Long Beach," but Kathleen was too busy with her teaching assignment in Arizona. Though Kathleen moved back to Long Beach in 1924, it was too late. Ingersoll was ill. He died in 1926. However, in 1927 when Walter Case wrote his historical and biographical history of Long Beach, he incorporated the early history written by Bessie, becoming chapters 1-9 of his 2-volume work.

Her work lives on and her achievements as a local historian are still appreciated. In the 1930s her image became one of the WPA's "green" faces found around campus at Poly High School. The faces are arranged in columns of five, placed on each side of doorways. One, on the second story administration building, depicts Miguel de Cervantes and Mark Twain, Euclid and both David Burcham, the school's principal, and Jane (Bessie) Harnett.

Tom and His Mill

I often tease my oldest brother Tom by telling him not to be too fussy about having so many sisters. I remind him he might easily have had eleven sisters since Mother lost twin girls somewhere between Ethel and Josie.

Tom was industrious and looked to the future. He knew farmers needed millers to process grain for bread and to feed animals. With the growth of farming in the area he decided opportunities lay ahead for a milling company. In 1897, at the young age of 22, he bought a share in the Lillard and Taylor grist mill, which was then located at 237 Olive. He later purchased the entire business, changing the name to the Long Beach Milling Company.

The business boomed with the opening of the Los Alamitos Sugar Factory in 1899, with farmers raising sugar beets swamping him with orders for feed for their animals. The firm also delivered feed to the dairies and chicken ranches in the area. In 1905, Tom moved the growing company to a site fronting on Broadway, Cerritos and Appleton (1058 Appleton) where the Southern Pacific extended a spur line to the milling company.

When the city decided to remove the rail tracts from Broadway in 1922, Tom, realizing he needed rail access, moved. The company's new home was at 2785 American Avenue. It was above a lake that stretched from the milling company's new location all the way to Willow Street. It was later drained. This site remained the company's home until Tom retired and closed the business on his 78th birthday, in October 1952. The land is now occupied by Long Beach Memorial Hospital.

Tom never married and I used to say he was wedded to his business. For more than ten years I worked in the office and of all the funny things that came up, our Blackie was the source of most of them. Blackie being our well-loved cat.

101

Being a milling company there were thousands of sacks of wheat, barley, corn and oats stacked in the huge warehouse. One might guess that all this grain would bring rats and mice galore and naturally we populated the warehouse with cats by the dozens to take care of this situation. These cats entertained us all, and lovingly fed milk by the warehousemen who felt the felines needed a supplement to their rodent diet.

In September 1939, the company experienced a horrific fire in the middle of the night. It centered in the warehouse and the fire department had a hard time soaking mountains of flaming sacks of grain. It made a horrible mess and a terrible smell. Finally, after two weeks of insurance company red tape, we were allowed to begin cleaning up. I must admit the smell of sour, wet grain nearly did me in.

The night of the fire every cat left. Blackie was the only cat that had the courage to return. Some may have sneaked back and decided they could not stand such a smelly place, not knowing as we did that time eventually would change things. But they never came back. From then on, every cat and kitten was related to Blackie and she ruled the warehouse like a queen. No strange male cat was ever allowed in the place. She made her visits to the outside world when and where she pleased but she did not permit any friends into the warehouse.

As the years passed, the warehouse gradually became well populated with Blackie's progeny. Blackie was a stern but protective mother. When clients brought in dogs to the store attached to the warehouse, Blackie made sure they kept away from any kittens. Three times she attacked a dog and Tom picked up the veterinary bill for the dog. After one last big bill, Tom forbid Blackie coming into the store section of the plant. Everyone kept an eye out to see that she wouldn't attack any more dogs.

I felt it wrong that the kittens would never know what a dog looked like and decided to do something about it. I got a toy dog we used to display dog collars and sweaters, and took it back to the warehouse to show Blackie's latest batch of kittens. The kittens were playing around their pans of milk and water, but Blackie was nowhere to be seen. The kittens were interested in the toy dog and to make it seem more real, I started to bark. It didn't bother the kittens but it brought Blackie down from the balcony hissing. With uncanny precision she landed exactly upon the back of the toy dog and they both fell over into a pan of nearby milk. Blackie soon realized the dog was not real after she dug her claws into its side. She gave me an indignant look as she regally lifted herself out of the pan of milk. She sat there dripping milk as well as indignation. She was so angry with me I couldn't help but laugh. My laughter brought others to the scene who also began to laugh. One workman was so bowled over with hysterical laughter, after seeing the milk sodden Blackie and the look on her face, that he rolled over and over on a stack of sacked wheat with such a belly laugh I can hear it to this day!

When I had sufficiently recovered, I picked up the display dog and left Blackie in a fury which possessed her for several days. It is a wonder she ever forgave me but as time went on we became friends again. One day she came into the office and announced that she was about to give birth once again. She started by jumping onto my desk with a "meow, meow, meow." Then went over to my brother-in-law Oscar's desk and gave Oscar the same bit of cat talk. Then she proceeded to Tom's desk, and Tom turned to me and said, "Ivy, this is the day. She's telling us. Keep an eye on her." It was her day and I knew she wanted me to know she counted on me for help if she needed it. I knew then that she had completely forgiven me for the horrible joke I had played on her.

Each new batch of kittens had to be trained to catch rats as well as mice. One morning Oscar's grandson came to the office with his mother and I thought he would enjoy seeing Blackie. I took the young lad out to find her. There she was at one end of the open drain pipe seeing to it that three kittens sharpened their claws before their rat catching lesson began. As we watched, one kitten was sent through the drain pipe while two other sharp clawed kittens waited at the other end. With Blackie beside them no rat would get away.

One morning Blackie came in and found Tom standing at the water cooler with a cup of water. She was evidently sure in her cat mind that anything Tom would be drinking must be something she'd relish and she stood at his feet begging and begging. Tom kept telling her she wouldn't want it but she wasn't convinced. She left him, went outside and before Tom had left the water cooler, she returned with a big fat rat and laid it at his feet. Well, if he wouldn't give it to her, she'd pay for it!

As the years passed, Blackie became more and more loved, a part of our milling company family. One morning my brother-in-law Oscar Morris and Ray Hubbard came in with the mail from the post office. They anxiously asked where Blackie was. No one had seen her. This was strange. She was usually around, greeting the truck drivers and warehouse and milling men by 8:30 in the morning. Oscar said he was afraid it was Blackie he saw lying in the middle of Willow Street. Complete silence reigned. I was ready to cry. One milling man looked out the window so none would see his tears. It was a horrible shock to all of us. Two of the workmen walked down to Willow and retrieved her body. She was gently returned to her realm and quietly buried. She was dreadfully missed.

Tom operated the company for 57 years and employed many including Oscar Morris, who married our sister Helen in 1912. In 1954 Tom had elective surgery, but didn't recover from the operation. Cause of death was listed as lobar pneumonia. I am sure those that had already passed on, and Blackie, were waiting on the other side to greet him.

The Lure of Alaska

One of the frequent visitors to our house was William Arthur Kersting, who liked to be called by his middle name. His was a handsome young Englishman who had recently arrived in the United States from London. Friends we had in common had told him to look us up. Gold had first been discovered in Alaska in 1880 (though the "big" discovery came in 1896) and Arthur decided that was where his future lay. However, he did make trips back to California and we never knew when he might show up on our doorstep. Once he arrived on a Saturday afternoon and it was a shock to him and to us when he entered our huge kitchen which was our bathroom on Saturday afternoons.

In the center of the kitchen was an enormous bath tub – some ten feet long, four feet wide and two feet deep. Two youngsters at a time frolicked in this, their combination bath and swimming pool. When Arthur made his unexpected appearance, he found three or four other Harnetts in various stages of dress and undress. An embarrassed Arthur backed out of the door onto the back porch with a very red face. It was still red after he got his breath and met Mother in the living room. He decided the front of the house was far safer for a young bachelor.

As time went on neighbors began to think Bessie was the reason for his steady visits. A man who mined in Alaska was a romantic figure to talk about in the rather mundane social life of Signal Hill, Burnett and Long Beach. All felt that Bessie would be doing well. She was noted for being a bit aloof, though, with her brilliant mind and beauty she was much sought after.

Arthur was away for two years in Alaska and when he returned our beautiful sister Ethel had come from England to join the family. She and our brother Jack had finished their educations and journeyed to America in October 1896. By this time Ellis Island had opened and they regaled us with tales of their Atlantic crossing and relatives left behind. I believe they travelled second class, for first and second class passengers did not have to undergo the inspection process at Ellis Island. Instead, these passengers received a cursory inspection aboard the ship; theory being that if a person could afford to purchase a first or second class ticket they were affluent and less likely to become a public charge in America due to medical or legal reasons. Years later Ethel and Jack said they were lucky they hadn't come the following year when a fire burned the immigration station completely to the ground.

When Jack and Ethel finally arrived in Long Beach, they found they had two new sisters, Kathleen and myself, with another sibling on the way. It took a while to get used to having them around since they had been separated from the rest of the family for seven years. However, it soon appeared that this young girl of eighteen was making a real impression not only on the family but upon Arthur Kersting.

One day I was in the kitchen behind the opened door, hidden from view. I was trying to sneak a sample of gingerbread that Ethel had labored to make. Before I could snatch a taste, Mother came in the back door with Arthur. The conversation was meant to be private, but I couldn't help but overhear that Arthur wanted to marry Ethel. I was all ears! As was the custom in those days he was first asking her mother and father for her hand in marriage.

The day wore on until all came home from school, had dinner and the children went to bed. Caroline and I slept together and loved to share stories after lights went off. Bessie's room adjoined ours. She had slipped in to see that we were all right just in time to hear me whisper to Caroline "Arthur's going to marry Ethel." Bessie was so amused she left quickly, smothering a laugh. She was off to her school teaching early in the morning before she could take the matter up with Mother.

All went to school except Kathleen, baby Frank and myself – all too young to attend. That evening Arthur was our guest at dinner. Before the entire table I opened my mouth with my choice bit of news and announced "Arthur's going to marry Ethel." Utter silence reigned. Caroline was shocked that I had done it. Arthur had the face of a ripened beet. Ethel left the room. I didn't see her face. I wasn't looking at her. Arthur engulfed my attention. He really looked as if something awful was going to happen to him. I had never seen a man explode but I thought he certainly might and I wanted to miss no part of it.

Arthur left the table in pursuit of Ethel. I guess he thought he should propose directly. Mother and Bessie somehow got things calmed down and dinner finished. Ethel accepted his proposal with the approval of Mother and Father.

The two were married in our home on February 2, 1899, not long after my eighth birthday. They settled in Baker, Oregon, for a while, where Arthur was proprietor of a lodge and where son William was born in 1901. By 1904 they were back in Long Beach, where daughter Gertrude entered the scene in 1904. Arthur worked in real estate, Ethel with the telephone company. They lived nearby at 643 Nevada, Long Beach.

Arthur and his stories of Alaska enthralled me, Norah and Josie. Norah and Josie were, like Bessie, school teachers. Each dreamt that one day they too might venture to the frozen north and have their own adventures.

On August 14, 1912, at age 27, Norah began her journey to Ketchikan, Alaska. Two weeks earlier an elaborate "farewell" was sponsored by the Burnett PTA, to honor this favorite teacher and wish her well. The Federation of Missionary Societies of Long Beach also held a reception for her. In Alaska she would teach native and minority children, working with Reverend Peter Roe who established the school. Fortunately, she left behind a diary which I have been able to use to fill in my story.

When Norah arrived at Ketchikan on August30, 1912, she found a town hidden behind Pennock Island, nestled among the mountains with a sizable population of 1600. It had several large buildings including the city hall, hotel, salmon cannery and a lumber mill. She later found Ketchikan was segregated into "Indian Town" and "White Town." For centuries it served as a summer fish camp for Tlingit natives before the "White Town" was established in 1885.

In 1905 a mission house was built, which in 1909 became the Yates Memorial Hospital. In 1912 it had two nurses but the indigenous Tlinglit population was hesitant to come. A few days after Norah arrived a native woman went into labor and the child died. The woman had refused to come to the hospital.

The town was a melting pot of all nationalities — one in every ten was Scandinavian, but there were also many Asians. Now Norah was to teach in the new school for native children and other minorities not allowed into the "white" school. On September 9, 1912, Norah started with only ten students, seven girls and three young boys. By October the class size had increased to twenty-five and Norah found herself teaching five grades. It was made more difficult because several of the young children did not understanding English. One of her projects was to set up a pen pal exchange with students at the Burnett school in Long Beach.

Children today would find it hard to believe that Ketchikan students and their teacher had to gather wood for the fire that kept them warm, keep the fire going and make sure their school was clean. They scrubbed floors and walls, did dishes in the kitchen attached to the school, and numerous other chores. Norah even spanked them if they misbehaved.

Sometimes unorthodox methods were used to make sure Native American students attended school. Houses were given numbers and each child given a tin badge to wear around their neck with the house number on it. Daily, the teacher noted the house number of each student and if some were missing the native police officer was contacted. The officer then went to the house and fined, and sometimes imprisoned, the father, if the child continued to skip school! I'm not sure that was the way Norah kept track of her students, but it was certainly an effective way of getting children to school.

Within a month Norah had numerous suitors. Dances were a pleasant pastime, and Norah attended many with Mr. Hale, who she described as a "religious individual" who sang in the choir. Not to be outdone, Mr. Barthelsen, also competing for a chance with Norah, attended the dances, later confessing he didn't know how to dance. Instead, he was soon asking her to any movies showing in town. She found Mr. Duffy, an Irishman, a great conversationalist and dancer. However, she quickly dismissed his advances when he told her he detested Indians, but to please her he did take off his hat to every other one Norah knew when she agreed to walk with him through town.

As the men competed for her affections, she was given candy, ice cream, fudge and donations of money for school supplies. She also made friends with the natives, visiting their homes and setting up basketry and quilting get togethers at the school. She was often called on to help at the hospital when one of the nurses got sick. She quickly learned how to dispense medicine, apply a plaster cast (a very messy job), help with amputations and deal with death. Here at the hospital, there was no racism, all were welcome.

Norah did not remain single for very long. It was a tall, 30-year-old, brown haired, grey eyed logger, William (Bill) Roy Selfridge, a partner and manager of the Sawyers and Reynolds Lumber Company, that won her heart. They married on November 24, 1914, in Alaska, then left for a six-week honeymoon, visiting Long Beach and other places along the Pacific. Sadly, their first born, Thomas died ten days after his birth in 1915. The valve in his stomach was not functioning properly and he was not getting nourishment. Norah and Bill had six more children — William, Anne, Ethel, John, and twins Richard and Robert. The children were reared and attended school in Alaska, visiting Long Beach whenever they could.

In 1928 Bill became a member of the Alaska Game Commission, and was elected chairman in 1931, a position he held until his resignation in 1935 when he became a game warden. Norah and Bill moved to Seattle following WWII and later back to southern California. Bill passed away in 1962, Norah in 1963. They are buried at Forest Lawn, Long Beach.

In July 1919, Josie, like Norah, decided to venture further afield and accepted a teaching position in Tenakee Village, Sitka District, Alaska. According to what Josie was told, the school was established in 1917 with ten white students between the ages of 6 and 20. It would certainly be an adventurous undertaking to teach at such a recently founded institution.

Tenakee Village was on the north shore of Tenakee Inlet on Chichagof Island about 45 miles from Juneau. Here miners from the interior goldfields, packers, trappers, prospectors and hangers-on came to winter rather than go south. Some stayed because they hadn't made enough money to go farther and some because they were avoiding the law or families they'd left behind. Tenakee living was cheap, with venison, seafood, homebrew, and free hot baths in the hot springs the area was known for. However, winter accommodations were limited and many were forced to live on their boats or in tents.

There Josie met James Jerome Simmons, who lived only a few houses away. I believe he worked in the cannery at the Tenakee Fisheries Company and had a permanent residence as did Josie. I don't think Josie was prepared for the conditions she found in Tenakee. Though there was a school, classes were held in various locations with funding for a "regular" school building not approved until 1922. However, she did find James.

Thirty-six-year-old Josie and forty-four-year-old James married February 8, 1920, in Sitka, the capital of Alaska during Russian ownership. Mother and Kathleen were planning to visit both Norah and Josie in June, but received a surprise on the eve of their departure when Josie and James wired they were on route to visit them, hoping to stay the entire summer. They stayed much longer, Josie giving birth to daughter Kathleen Elizabeth on May 6, 1921, just 2 days after my brother Edward's wife, Charlotte, delivered a baby girl, Jean Frances. James and Josie decided conditions in Tenakee were not conducive to raising children and stayed in southern California. In 1922 they had another child who they christened Ernest.

James worked as a stevedore at the Port of Los Angeles and later, as the Great Depression worsened, Josie resumed teaching. Remembering how the family so loved to put on plays, she instilled in her fifth-grade students at Bandini Street School in San Pedro a love of acting as well as learning. Instead of social studies reports being dull and uninteresting facts, she added dramatization. Students in her classroom were divided into groups and assigned a topic which they researched, wrote a script for and then performed. She made learning fun.

What about me, Ivy? Having caught the "Alaska bug," I went to Ketchikan, Alaska, in August 1916 and lived a year with Norah. Norah had written how she was asked to take on hospital duties, in addition to teaching, when nurses Wygnant or Barlow were sick.

There were dressings to make, wards to clean, and patients to take care of. She told me how she tried to remain calm when a 17-year-old boy handed her his glass eye. She had no idea what to do with it and neither did Nurse Barlow, until they finally decided to put it in the instrument case for safe keeping. I thought I would be of use in faraway Alaska, helping in whatever way I could.

My experiences in Ketchikan, and the need of medical care for returning World War I veterans, led me to seek a career in nursing. I had aspirations of becoming a nurse, like my mother had been to her father. When I heard Seaside Hospital was starting a nurse training program in 1918, I enrolled in the three-year course. But back problems prevented me from continuing in the medical profession. Instead, I helped take care of Mother, worked for Tom in his mill and feed store, and also as his housekeeper and, later, as his nurse.

Romance never found me. Perhaps I was too religious and it scared suitors. When my brother Jack was very ill, his wife Leonora telephoned me saying he might not live through the night. The next morning, I went to church with Jack very much on my heart and in my prayers. As I knelt by the altar rail a great white light surrounded me. It was a very beautiful moment and when it was over, I was at peace. All was well with my world. I reached home and found Jack was well and out of danger. This was just one instance in which I felt a spiritual presence which responded to my prayers.

Romance in Eureka

Jack left Long Beach for Eureka, California, around 1903 after getting a job with the newly formed North Mountain Power Company, supplying electrical power to the many industries in Humboldt Bay.

Eureka was a booming, progressive city and the company wanted to create a hydroelectric system near Weaverville, with connecting power lines to Eureka. The lines went over some of the most rugged terrain imaginable, and Jack was often out in the field solving logistics problems.

Here, in Eureka, my 30-year-old brother married 25-year-old Leonora Bandy on July 2, 1908. Leonora, a beautician, had moved to the growing town a few years earlier from Illinois. I believe the pair may have met at one of the Bachelor Girls parties, where Leonora's singing and dramatic performances must have reminded Jack of home and his sisters, who were members of the Bachelor Girls of Signal Hill. Jack and Leonora kept their marriage plans secret and only the Episcopalian minister and two witnesses were in attendance.

My brother Edward also moved to Eureka, and found a wife.

When Edward graduated from high school in 1906, he worked in the city engineer's department as a surveyor before moving north to join Jack in 1909. There he worked for the Western State Gas and Electric Company as a lineman before he was drafted in 1918. In 1914 he married Charlotte Georgeson, a native of Scotland, who had been living in Eureka since 1907, making a home with her uncle, Fred W. Georgeson, a banker and founding member of the Save the Redwoods League.

The war and the devastating family tragedies of 1918, drove both Jack, Edward and their families back to Long Beach. On May 1st, houses and properties sold, they headed south to a home bereft of a sister and father.

Edward was soon drafted, but Jack, was too old to be called up. By the guidelines set down by the 1917 Selective Service Act, all males aged 21 to 30 were required to register to potentially be selected for military service. At the request of the War Department, Congress amended the law in August 1918 to expand the age range to include all men 18 to 45, and to bar further volunteering. Jack was now "of age" to register, which he did in September 1918. Fortunately, the war ended in November and Jack was never "called up."

I guess you could say Jack also caught "gold fever," like his sisters, though it was Californian gold, not Alaskan. Jack soon heard of an opportunity in the gold town of Hammonton in Yuba County, whose gold was needed in the war effort. Assured by the family that they could manage without him, he and Leonora headed north.

Hammonton, settled in 1903, was one of the most extensively drilled areas in the United States and was notably one of the top ten gold producing districts in America. Here Jack worked as chief electrician for the Yuba Consolidated Gold Fields, a dredger company, which perfected large-scale bucket-line dredging into one of the most efficient methods for mining placer gold.

Unable to have children, Leonora and Jack adopted baby Edwin Abbott in 1919, while living in Hammonton. In 1920 they changed the child's name to James Everett Harnett.

In November 1921, the family decided to move back to Long Beach because of Jack's ill health and to be closer to family. Jack's medical issues soon improved and in February 1922 he went to work for the S. and H. Electrical Company in Alhambra. By 1924 Jack's family had relocated to the Belvedere area of East Los Angeles where Jack formed his own company Belvedere Service Electric Company.

Marrying a Cowboy

Anne was the artistic one on the family. In June 1903, she graduated from Long Beach High School, attended Throop Polytechnic Institute (later to become Cal Tech) in Pasadena, and California School of Fine Arts in San Francisco. Before resuming her studies in San Francisco, she worked for Ernest Batchelder making art tiles at his kiln house and School of Arts and Crafts in Pasadena. We always liked to visit the Chocolate Shop (217 West 6th) in Los Angeles where we proudly told all we met that our sister Anne had worked on the Dutch tile murals in the shop, which she finished in 1914. (Editor's note: to see these tiles, follow this link: https://la.curbed.com/2016/8/10/12405422/los-angeles-batchelder-dutch-chocolate-shop-3d)

Anne was another in the family who wanted to see the world. In 1917 her wanderlust got her as far as San Francisco, where she furthered her art education by studying at the California School of Fine Arts.

An art commission in 1920 brought her to Colorado. Here she met widower Frank Winthrop Kimball who was staying in Denver while his children attended high school. Frank was twenty-six years older than Anne, but she was drawn to him and his colorful life. They both shared a common bond — 1918 — which was a bad year for both. Anne had lost her father as well as her sister, Bessie.

Frank lost his wife, Grace.

Frank was certainly an interesting man. Frank and his trapper father Hiram travelled down the Mississippi River when Frank was a boy in the 1870s. The tales he had to tell of his journey rivaled those of Mark Twain. When Frank was about 19 or 20, he traveled from Wisconsin to Colorado, and then to Montana and Wyoming, where he worked as a cowboy. He was trail boss in charge of delivering a herd of cattle to the Standing Rock Agency in 1890 for the government to issue to Sitting Bull. While working on the Powder River in Montana, he trekked to Wyoming and found the spot he wanted to homestead.

Anne married this man right out of a Dime Western on October 2, 1920, in Colorado. Their first child, Jane Caroline, was born in Denver August 1, 1921. When Anne's step children finished school Frank, Anne and baby Jane moved to Frank's cattle ranch near Aladdin, Wyoming. Here daughter Dorothy entered the world in 1923 and son Edward in 1925.

Asthma, which both Anne and Frank suffered from, led them to sell the ranch in 1927. They relocated to Flagstaff, Arizona, where son John was born the following year. Frank's health improved, but Anne's got worse. In the midst of the Depression, 1932, they moved to San Bernardino, California, to live with Frank's daughter from his first marriage, Katharine.

After only one year in California, Frank had to repossess the Wyoming ranch, since the buyer couldn't continue to make payments. The family moved back to Wyoming. Frank died in 1949; Anne, who split her time between Long Beach and Aladdin where two of Anne's children remained, passed away in 1975. Both Anne and Frank are buried on the Kimball homestead ranch near Aladdin, Crook County, Wyoming.

Our Youngest Brothers

Late in the summer of 1918, our brothers Edward and Frank were serving in World War I, called the Great War back then. Jack had registered for the draft while working as a civil engineer for the Yuba Consolidated Gold Fields. His draft number was never called. Tom never registered, claiming his milling business was too important for the war effort for him to be drafted, besides at age 44 he was pretty close to being exempt anyway, the age limit being 45. During the war, Charlotte, Edward's wife, lived with us at 730 Sunrise Boulevard.

There must have been some eleven or twelve of us at home one particular evening. Anne and I were bathing in the downstairs bathroom — one just out and the other just in the tub. We heard running about upstairs, down the stairs, and back and forth into the kitchen. When we shouted "what's the matter!" we got no answer, only more running about. Finally, Anne opened the bathroom door and shrieked at the top of her lungs, "WHAT IS THE MATTER!" just as Charlotte ran through the downstairs hall. She heard Anne and to our horror she shouted back, "The house is on fire!" This shocked and frightened us into action. Grabbing towels for covering we dashed out terrified. Anne tried to think of what we ought to save and decided upon our huge family Bible. She headed for the library at the foot of the stairs, with me dripping close behind.

At the foot of the stairs, we tried to get some idea of what was going on. We saw Tom in the upstairs hall, but he only gave us a look as he went into Mother's room. Suddenly it dawned on us that there was no smell of smoke and we decided Mother must be very ill. When we caught a glimpse of Josie in the upstairs hall we finally got her attention and she said, "Hurry and come on up. Edward is home!" We quickly put on more appropriate attire for this thrilling moment of a visit from one of our soldier brothers.

Edward was being sent from Camp Lewis in Washington State down to Camp Kearney near San Diego and had the opportunity for a brief visit. We all wished Los Angeles had succeeded in locating the camp close to the City of Angels, which meant we would have Edward closer. But that was not to be. The government chose San Diego and created a camp from a dry desolate area. The brush and sand mesas were so far out in the country that long after taps, soldiers were serenaded with coyotes. A sound that reminded Edward of his youth in Long Beach.

During the war, Edward served in a machine gun corps and afterwards worked for the Long Beach Shipbuilding Company. Leaving the shipbuilding company, he joined the Long Beach Engineering Department. One story he loved to tell was about a fellow who came into the City Engineer's office and the two got to talking. The customer asked, "By the way, do you know Tom Harnett and Frank Harnett?" Edward said, "just distantly. Dr. Frank was the youngest of 14, and I was the 10th; Tom was the 2nd so I was just distantly related."

During the Depression Edward and his family lived with Tom and me in the big 14-room home at 730 Sunrise Boulevard. Edward was under very heavy pressure having to take on two jobs, heading the Engineering Department and Public Service departments, both having to deal with the aftermath of the 1933 earthquake damage. He assumed both roles on November 17, 1934.

On January 20, 1935, Edward played a game of tennis and later had a serious attack of angina pectoris, a symptom of coronary artery disease. By seven o'clock that evening my brother was dead.

It was one of those attacks that can take one in 24 hours. My sister Ethel had a similar attack in 1962 and, like Edward, was gone within 24 hours. Neither of them had ever had any previous heart problems. The Engineering and Public Service departments, which Edward had headed for such a short while, planted a memorial Oriental sycamore in Edward's honor in Recreation Park a few months later.

The family has many fond memories of Edward. Tom's business telephone was 13 — since he had the thirteenth telephone installed in Long Beach, one of 16 original subscribers. One afternoon the telephone rang and Tom was told that Edward had had a bad accident on his bicycle and would Tom please come to the undertaker's home at once. Tom drove to the high school to get Bessie to go with him. As they arrived, the "dead wagon" stood at the roadside. Tom and Bessie steeled themselves for the worst. One went to an undertakers only to make arrangements for the dead.

Edward's bicycle chain had broken as he was riding up Atlantic Avenue. He was thrown and picked up unconscious by the driver of the "dead wagon" who was on his way to the undertakers. So, Edward was delivered to the McFadgen's Parlors along with a body. It was a very thankful Tom and Bessie who brought Edward home — lying flat on his back in the carriage with his poor head in Bessie's lap.

There were many things to be burned in those early years, including trash. On one trash burning day, Father sent Edward to the house for matches. Edward, like many small boys, loved matches and the flame they made. He lit one or two on his way back to Father but dropped one that hadn't quite gone out. A barnyard isn't exactly the place to drop lighted matches. In no time the straw caught fire and ran its swift trail to the haystack. Then the alarm was sounded and panic set in.

Josie was sent to tell Mr. Myers, a neighbor on the northwest side of Willow and Atlantic. Mother had told her Mr. Myers had a bad heart and to go quietly to him and tell him very calmly that our barn was on fire. Josie knocked on his door and slowly and quietly said, "Mr. Myers can you please come and help us. Our barn is burning." She had followed Mother's instructions to the letter not to get him excited for fear of a heart attack.

Norah was sent to the 40-acre orange ranch where the Moores lived in a three-story house overlooking the whole of Long Beach. There was quite a rise up hill to the home. Norah was already frightened out of her wits thinking our whole place could soon burn to the ground. She rushed up the hill, breathless when she met Mr. Moore who, knowing something awful was in store for him, had to wait for her to get her breath. I am told that when they returned (probably having run all the way) Mr. Moore told the neighbors to tear down all the corrals adjoining the big barn to keep the fire from getting to the barn. It was his advice which helped save our barn.

There were helpful neighbors on all sides on 5, 10, 20, 30 and 40 acre ranches. The Clovers, the Saunders, the Shrodes, the Butlers and the Moore families all came to help. No one thought to call the fire department. Telephones were rare and to get word to them meant one would have to go by horse or bicycle. It would have taken at least a half hour to reach the fire department, 2.5 miles away. The fire horses would need to be harnessed and another half hour consumed in getting to the fire — up and down hill on Atlantic Avenue. By then the fire would have spread.

Our neighbor Mary Clover, who helped at the fire, told me years later she was so frightened she was able to haul a big wagon outside our barn to safety single handed. She didn't know where she got the strength. Other neighbors led animals to safety, and we didn't lose a single animal. If the fire had reached the hay loft, that would have been the end. Neighbors were neighbors in those days and helped rebuild and put things back into working order.

One thing, too funny to omit, was that one sister was in the bathtub when "all hell broke loose in our back yard." She rushed outside wrapped only in a towel, and was met by Mary Clover who told her the fire was behind the barn and if she hurried she would have time to go back and get her clothes on!

I still remember chasing rabbits with Edward. A little wooden sluice or drain across the road that led up to the Moore's three-story home on their 40-acre orange ranch across the street from our home. Rabbits sometimes hid in it and Edward and I would find and catch them and raise them. We soon learned that we could stop a jack rabbit in his run by whistling a long low whistle. He would sit up on his hind legs, lift his ears high and look to see where the noise came from. Poor rabbits, I know they would rather have been free, but we took good care of them.

After Edward's death Charlotte and the children stayed with us for four years. Their children, Jean and Stanley, were only 12 and 10 when their father died. They were like my own children and I have fond memories of them as well as their father. I often took walks with Jean and her friends to Reservoir Hill, or "little hill" as we called it. We usually planned it for an hour when the train would be passing under the Willow Street bridge, so she, like her aunts and uncles before her, might stand there on the bridge and enjoy being frightened by whistles and billowing smoke.

One day, after wandering over the hill gathering wildflowers, Jean, Julia Morris and Camilla and Perry Austin came dashing over the brow of the hill, excitedly exclaiming, "We found an ostrich." I was not sure to believe them but hurried over to the east side of the hill top with them to see what all their excitement was about.

There in a large pen, much like a horse corral, was an enormous ostrich. We gaped in wonder and he at us. The president of an oil company, whose family lived in the vicinity of Taft in the Central Valley, had small children and this ostrich had been their favorite pet until it grew and began to use its heavy feet too violently, kicking them with sometimes serious consequences. It was decided Reservoir Hill was the safest spot to put this once beloved pet and Jean and her friends claimed him as their own and so he became. The children brought him oranges, and much to our delight Battling Rudy, which was his name we learned from a newspaper account, loved them. Braver and braver they became in feeding the Valencia oranges to him until one of the children let him take an orange from an open palm.

Rudy was always so happy to see them, even me, and especially the oranges. We would watch with wonder as he gulped a whole orange creating a fascinating bulge the entire length of his long neck. When he finished, he would run towards us in his pen, spread his wings, rest them and his long neck on the ground in a thank-you bow.

Then came the day when Battling Rudy laid an egg. Fifteen years he had lived as a monarch upon his hill top before his owners discovered him to be a SHE. That afternoon my friend's son Perry was writing a letter to his grandmother: "Aunt Ivy just came in and says that after fifteen years she laid an egg." No mention was made of Battling Rudy and Mrs. Waterman was really puzzled over the letter!

Frank was born in 1897, when Mother was 49 and Father 57. The last of the Harnett clan. Many of the family were away, except for 3-year-old Kathleen and myself. That summer Helen, Norah, Anne, Edward and Josie had gone to Glendale to help the Gulvins on their fruit ranch. They harvested the fruit and prepared it for market, while Josie helped Mrs. Gulvin in the house.

In June 1897, they received a letter from home telling them of the arrival of a new baby. When they told Mr. Gulvin that his name was Frank, he said, "If he is anything like his Uncle Frank, he will be a fine man indeed." Mr. Gulvin remembered Father's brother, Frank, from Mr. Gulvin's days at our farm in Kent. My other siblings went home before Josie did and she did not see Frank until he was about two months old, a darling blue-eyed infant.

While he was still a baby, Frank became seriously ill. I believe the doctor called it brain fever, but I think I was told years later that was the name given to a mastoid, which could lead to hearing loss, blood clots, meningitis, or a brain abscess. At any rate, he was very ill and lay moaning in bed, turning his head from side to side. Mother worked with him vigilantly and when he recovered the doctor told her it was only her nursing that brought him through.

I will never forget the night he walked through a bed of hot ashes left from a bonfire in the yard. Mother was supposed to sing in the choir that night but she spent her time walking with him or rocking him in response to his demands. After that experience he grew well, though he seemed a little frail for a time.

Then came the years when he was a very active boy among a group of sisters, for Edward, the next boy in age, was seven years older. Not wanting to play with girls, Frank began hanging out with a group of boys his own age who got into lots of mischief, including the 1905 Densmore Packing Company's hay stack fire.

The company managed a ten-acre pear, peach, apricot and apple tree fruit ranch. It was bordered by Willow Street on the north, California Avenue on the west, Orange Avenue on the east and Burnett Street on the south. The fruit was picked and packed on the spot — in a large cannery building. Since horses were needed for ploughing the orchard, a huge stack of baled hay was kept outside the west side of the cannery building next to the railroad.

There were two boys that Frank and a friend, Carol Adams, were not supposed to play with. That meant that Frank and Carol wanted to play with them even more. One afternoon these two boys, with Frank and Carol tagging along, decided to do something with the loose hay. They found a scoop shovel and placed the loose straw on it. One of the boys just happened to have matches in his pocket. It all went faster than anyone planned.

A breeze picked up more of the loose hay and like lightning the straw made its flaming path to the stack of bales. The boys knew they couldn't put the blaze out, and quickly disappeared. Men in the cannery rushed to the inferno. One quickly got on top of the bales and managed to maneuver the flaming bundles off to safe ground, before the others could ignite.

Mrs. Adams later contacted Mother and said she knew her son had nothing to do with it, for he had come home about 4 p.m. and immediately went to bed. Mother replied that so had had Frank. When she asked Frank what the problem was, he said he just felt ill. He didn't add it was because he felt sick because the hay caught on fire. He never confessed to the crime until years later, but Mother always felt Frank had a hand in it.

That was the nearest the group came to real trouble, though Frank did receive one spanking from the principal at Burnett school. It seemed Frank passed a note that he didn't write and the teacher confiscated it. It wasn't a very nice note. Besides getting the whipping in school, when he got home he received a second one.

Then came high school where Frank seemed to light heartedly slip through until graduation day when he was told in order to graduate he needed to learn to recite a German poem and turn in an English paper. With Bessie one of the teachers in high school it was embarrassing her brother was so slack in his school work. With her prodding he memorized part of the poem and with the kindness of his instructor, Mr. Bauman, he was given the rest of the summer of 1915 to learn the rest. He wrote his paper and Josie typed it for him and turned it in the day of graduation. That evening he was given a dummy diploma which was exchanged in the summer for a real one, after he had memorized his German poem.

Frank then went to work as a delivery man for a grocer and the next year went to college in Corvallis, Oregon, where he was accepted in spite of his low grades. One year passed and he was barely twenty-one, draft age for World War One. He enlisted and found himself stationed in Seattle, Washington, an officer in the Navy Air Force, wearing a forest green uniform. But his service was short for the Armistice was signed and he came home with the rank of Chief Quartermaster. He married Anna Mary Walters, his longtime sweetheart on June 29, 1920.

Their romance blossomed in 1914 at the home of the Butlers who owned an orange ranch on Willow, between Atlantic and California. One night there was a party at the home and when it was over Mrs. Butler asked Frank to take Anna Mary, who lived about four blocks from the Butlers, home.

Anna Mary and Frank shared a love of tennis and both were members of the Poly High tennis team. The club was quite active and in 1915 the two paired up and became mixed doubles champions.

Anna Mary lived one-half block south of the cemetery and the two would meet under a big tree in the cemetery where they spent their evenings. Once a month, they treated themselves by travelling to Los Angeles to see a film. They would walk ten blocks down to Willowville, on Willow Street, and catch the Pacific Electric and go the Orpheum Theater. They would stay until the show was over and end up at the chocolate shop which our sister, Anne, designed tiles for. The couple would then catch the last car to Long Beach at 12:15 a.m. and get off at Willowville about 1 a.m.

After the war, Frank worked at Tom's Long Beach Milling Company until Frank decided to become a chiropractor. In 1926, he graduated from the Los Angeles Chiropractic College and practiced for three years. In 1929, he closed his chiropractic practice and went to work for the newly organized Recreation Department, a job he held for more than thirty years. In 1932, he became Associate Director of the department, retiring in 1962.

In 1948, he joined the Long Beach Mounted Police, a group of horsemen that led the Rose Parade for years, twelve of which included Frank and his horse, Buster. In 1954, when Frank was their president, the Long Beach Mounted Police were asked to be in Michael Todd's movie, "Around the World in 80 Days." In one scene, the extras were told to throw confetti at the riders, which frightened the horses and resulted in near pandemonium.

GENERAL THEATRICAL FUND.

The Nobility, Gentry, and Public in general, are most respectfully informed that the SEVENTH ANNIVERSARY of the above Institution will be celebrated by a PUBLIC DINNER at the London Tavern, Bishopsgate-street, on MONDAY, the 6th of APRIL, 1846,

CHARLES DICKENS, Esq., in the Chair.

FIRST LIST OF VICE-PRESIDENTS.

His Grace the Duke of Northumberland, K.G.
The Right Hon. the Earl Fitzhardinge.
The Right Hon. Lord Francis Egerton, M.P.
Hon. Francis Henry Fitzhardinge Berkeley, M.P.
Sir Bellingham Graham, Bart
Thomas Slingsby Duncombe, Esq., M.P.
B. B. Cabbell, Esq., F.R.S., F.S.A.
Mr. Serjeant Talfourd, F.R.S.

A. Archdeckne, Esq.
J. Elliotson, Esq., M.D.
R. Feast, Esq.
Luke James Hansard, Esq.
William Henry West Betty, Esq.
James Davidson, Esq.
Henry F. Richardson, Esq.
G. Cruikshank, Esq.
Benjamin Webster, Esq., Theatre Royal, Haymarket.
Robert Bell, Esq.
Peter Berrell, Esq., M.R.C.S.E.

E. Brewster, Esq.
Charles Cochrane, Esq.
Henry Collingwood Ibbetson, Esq.
Edward Culliford, Esq.
T. P. Cooke, Esq.
William Kiddle, Esq.
Charles Manby, Esq.
D. W. Osbaldiston, Esq.
Philip Salomons, Esq.
A. W. Hoggins, Esq.

The musical arrangements will be under the direction of Mr. J. L. Hatton, assisted by the following eminent vocal and instrumental performers :—Madame Albertazzi, Miss Rainforth, Miss A. Williams, Miss M. Williams, Miss Emma Lucombe, Mrs. W. Weiss, Miss Mariott O'Connor; Mr. Richardson, M. Felix Godefroid, Mr. Hobbs, Mr. Bradbury, Mr. Weiss, Mr. Genge, Mr. Chapman, Mr. Lockey, Mr. Paul Bedford, Mr. Machin, Mr. Francis, Mr. J. W.

Peter Berrell, Ivy's grandfather, was a member of the London General Theatrical Fund along with Charles Dickens.
London Morning Post March 25, 1846

Dr. Peter Berrell worked as a surgeon at
New Bethlem Hospital, also known as Bedlam.
Courtesy of Wikipedia

The Milling Company's first location, 237 Olive. c. 1904.
Courtesy of the Long Beach History Collection, Long Beach Public Library

Josie, Helen, Mother Harnett, Kathleen, Charlotte
with various children. Family photo.

Jane Harnett, known in the family as Bessie.
Family photo.

Ivy at the Long Beach Pageant, 1915.
Family photo.

Ivy as a student nurse, 1918.
Family photo.

Jack and son Jim at Long Beach, c1920.
Family photo

Frank in first long pants, c1907.
Family photo.

Edward's military record.
Courtesy of the Long Beach History Collection, Long Beach Public Library

Kathleen's graduation from Berkeley, 1916. She was
the top graduating student. Family photo.

St. Luke's Episcopal Church, Fifth & Locust, c1900.
Courtesy of the Long Beach History Collection, Long Beach Public Library

Harnett family home on Sunrise. Now part of the
Sunrise Boulevard Historic District.
Source: C. Burnett

EPILOGUE

"They named her Ivy so she clung around the house." So Kathleen said. True or not, I did. Sisters and brothers grew up, got married and left the big family home at 730 Sunrise Boulevard. Fourteen rooms, a basement and a double garage all full to the bursting point. What does one do? Year by year as each member of this large family of fourteen children left, one by one, for married life or new fields of adventure, they left behind all sorts of belongings. Trunks full of them. Periodically Mother and I went through them, weeding out items the others seemed to no longer want.

Year by year the family dwindled until there was only Tom and Ivy. Ivy, who still, like her name, clung to the house. The house was too big for just two people and in 1944 Frank said he would buy the house from us and move his family into it. What release! Tom and I then moved to 4225 Gundry in 1945, where we stayed until 1951 when we purchased a home at 2301 Pasadena — a street that went right through our former ranch.

We had never imagined that one day we would be living on our former ranch property on Pasadena Avenue. It was now a city street with automobiles, trucks and trailers rushing up and down at all hours. There was also a city fire station with a chemical truck and a hook and ladder close by which would come shrieking up the street on its way to put out the fires in the now big city of Long Beach.

As I sit here writing on January 24, 1963, Josie is preparing to go to the Iowa Pork Shop for some bargains. Anne is sitting on her bed getting a faraway view of the painting she is currently working on. Norah is outside gardening. Kathleen is away doing volunteer work at St. Luke's.

I am happy Kathleen decided to move back to Long Beach two years ago and live with me, her 72-year-old sister. When she retired in 1955, she moved to Running Springs, but has made her way back to her roots. She was a teacher all her life, following in the footsteps of our sisters Bessie, Josie and Norah.

We were so proud of her when she graduated from U.C. Berkeley. We were also delighted when she won a Phoebe Hearst scholarship to Berkeley in 1915, which helped considerably with expenses. Even so we couldn't all afford to travel there for her special day, but we knew something special was about to happen after Professor Henry Morse Stephens wrote Bessie saying he wanted her to be sure to be there. This was difficult for Bessie, then a high school teacher, since it was the last month of the school year, but she managed to attend the ceremony.

Kathleen had been called before the Regents and informed the night before graduation that she was going to get the gold metal as the Most Distinguished Student among the 3,000 1916 graduates. She was overwhelmed, and was told to tell no one except her immediate family. But Kathleen was brimming with the news and after announcing to her roommates Dorothy and Elizabeth Webster, that they were "her immediate family," she told all. She was even happier when Bessie arrived the morning of the graduation to witness the presentation.

We saved the newspaper article about Kathleen's graduation which was in the May 24, 1916, *Los Angeles Herald.* It also appeared in other newspapers such as the *San Francisco Call.*

Miss Kathleen Harnett Heads the Graduating Class at the University of California

MISS KATHLEEN HARNETT of Long Beach was graduated at the University of California last week at the head of a class of over one thousand. How many years ago was it that it was considered unnecessary for a woman to know how to read and write unless she expected to be a school ma'am. Fifty years ago, Miss Harnett could not have graduated in any mixed class at any university in the world. Twenty-five years ago, she would have been held up to the public view as a sort of freak, like a meadow lark who could talk or a parrot who had learned to swim. Today she is the pride of California — and nobody ever thinks of explaining how she came to go to the university at all, or apologizing for the fact that she was graduated at the head of the class. And not one newspaper in the state of California has as yet put the palpitating question as to whether Miss Harnett intends to sing Greek 1 or Latin to while away the time when she's waiting for the dishwater to heat. "Amo —a mas —amat. Why it's as easy to learn as "enie, menie, minie, mo," when once you get the hang of it. Isn't it, Miss Harnett. But — whisper— have you ever heard of the eloquent sign in the suffrage parade in New York last year; "This comes from letting women learn to read" — thus ran the legend, and they do say that some of those who stood on the sidewalk to hiss the demonstration couldn't read the sign. And they hissed the loudest of all.

Yes, teaching was the only option open to this amazing sister of mine. Even with a degree in history and Spanish, and her honors from Berkeley, Kathleen could not get a teaching job in Long Beach. The school district was only accepting those with two years of experience, so in 1917 Kathleen moved to Morenci, Arizona, to teach high school. She returned to Long Beach in 1924 to teach Spanish and history at Poly High School where she eventually became head of the History Department.

Anne makes this her home when she isn't spending time with her children in Wyoming. Norah visits frequently from Whittier and Helen lives nearby.

Helen, the middle sister between Josie and Norah, was content to stay in Long Beach, marrying an Arkansas man, Oscar Morris on May 18, 1912. Oscar worked for Tom at the milling company, having joined the business in 1907 as a salesman. Helen worked there as a bookkeeper. The couple raised three children in Long Beach — John, Marguerite and Julia.

We miss our siblings who are no longer with us — Geoffrey, Caroline, Bessie, Ethel, Edward, Tom, and Jack, as well as Mother and Father and nieces and nephews who died too young.

We surviving sisters get together often and frequently venture out to explore the great U. S. of A. Kathleen drives. She's a pretty good driver, except for the time she ran into a Navy truck when we were on our way to a funeral. Three years ago Helen, Kathleen and I went on a marvelous 3-week road adventure through Arizona, Nevada, Utah and Colorado visiting our many relatives and finally picking up Anne in Wyoming for the return trip.

At Anne's home, we were impressed to see a big sign board with FK on it for Frank Kimball, the ranch which Anne's son Edward now runs. It was a 9 mile drive down a dirt road to finally get to the ranch house, where we were entertained that evening with cowboy music. Well worth the entire trip!

Being together brings back memories. We talk about Helen's daughter Julia's wedding in 1948. How Frank's family had already scheduled a vacation to Wyoming and would not be around for the ceremony. Then the trip fell through when the transmission in the car gave out just outside Las Vegas. Once the car was fixed, they decided to turn around and come back for the ceremony. However, Frank's daughter Polly was feeling a bit sad that she had no part in the wedding, but Julia found her a job assisting at the cake table and running errands. Her most important errand, Helen laughed, was Polly telling her cousin Stanley (Edward's son), to pull in his feet or else he would trip Julia as she walked down the aisle!

Some memories are not as pleasant, such as the 1933 Long Beach earthquake. I remember how I was almost crushed when a cabinet fell behind me as I fled down the back stairs. The banister became my savior, my hands clutching it to prevent me being thrown against the walls. Somehow, I avoided being hit by the bricks which flew about from our tall fireplace. Our nerves were shattered from days of subsequent quaking, but we had survived.

The earthquake was in March, but in June we had another terrifying experience. Cousin Ned Bolger and his Aunt Ecie were visiting us. I was asleep when a terrific explosion flung me from my bed. The house was shaking and I could see flames reflected on our neighbor's homes to the west and south of us. Logic told me that our house was on fire. But as I reached for the door knob to the kitchen, I realized it was not hot. In the kitchen I found Ned, Tom and Frank standing by the window watching the flames on Signal Hill.

It was a horrible tragedy that began with the tremendous blast at Richfield Oil, which was felt in cities thirty miles away. Kathleen, at her post at the high school, knew it must have been really bad for us and had a friend quickly drive her home only to find that no one was allowed to enter the area. Knowing the terrane, she climbed a high bank along the railroad right of way at the back of our home. She followed the path and broke down in tears of joy when she found our home still standing.

Coming to the front garden she saw we no longer had a front door — the huge oak door had split in half and been flung the length of the front hall. Halfway up the stairs the French doors were scrambled in a heap.

Fortunately, the heroic efforts of 500 men, including Ned, Tom and Frank, armed with shovels, prevented the oil that flowed from broken storage vats from igniting and spreading the fire into residential areas. Still, 9 people died and 25 were injured. It was later found that a storage tank at 27th and Lime, not far from our Sunrise Boulevard home, had caused the explosion.

In reliving that day, my sisters and I could not help but remember the past — the wild flowers, animals, farms, and families that made Signal Hill, the Burnett area and Long Beach such wonderous, different places before 1921, and the discovery of oil.

I hope this memoir will eventually be published and bring our memories to light. My wish is that it will allow readers an enjoyable vision of the Long Beach that once was and the family that grew with the city.

IVY'S POEM

"The Storm"
Published in the Poly High Yearbook,
The Caerulea in 1915:

The lightning streaks the southern sky,
Its forked fury lights the sea.
O'er rugged rocks the tide foams up
Seething and surging it rages in
With the noise of a monster
Aroused from his sleep.

Now torn from mossy beds beneath.
The helpless seaweed swirls about,
And flung on jagged cliffs whose teeth.
Sharpened through ages of stormy sea,
Tear it asunder,
And there let it lie.

Out on white-capped billows tossed,
This merciless tyrant conquers all.
It seizes ships and flings them high,
When like Charybdis* it sucks them down
While the thunder applauds
With its rumble and roar.

*In Greek mythology, Charybdis is a whirlpool off the coast of Sicily
personified in Greek mythology as a female monster.

EIGHTH GRADE EXAMINATION FOR GRAMMAR SCHOOLS, NOVEMBER, 1912

Spelling

Have someone read these words to you and see how many you can spell correctly. No Hints! You don't want to have to stand in the corner do you?

Exaggerate, incentive, conscious, pennyweight, chandelier, patient, potential, creature, participate, authentic, bequeath, diminish, genuine, vinegar, incident, monotony, hyphen, antecedent, autumn, hideous, relieve, conceive, control, symptom, rhinoceros, adjective, partial, musician, architect, exhaust, diagram, endeavor, scissors, associate, saucepan, benefit, masculine, synopsis, circulate, eccentric.

Arithmetic

1. Write in words the following: .5764; .000003; .123416; 65310965; 43.37
2. Solve: 35.7 plus 4, 5.8 plus 5.14 - 59.112
3. Find cost at 12 1/2 cents per sq. yd. of kalsomining the walls of a room 20 ft. long, 16 ft. wide and 9 ft. high, deducting 1 door 8 ft. by 4 ft. 6 in. and 2 windows 5 ft. by 3 ft. 6 in. each.
4. A man bought a farm for $2400 and sold it for $2700. What per cent did he gain?
5. A man sold a watch for $180 and lost 16 2/3 %. What was the original cost of the watch?
6. Find the amount of $50.30 for 3 yrs. 3 mo. and 3 days, at 8 per cent.

7. A school enrolled 120 pupils and the number of boys was two thirds of the number of girls. How many of each sex were enrolled?
8. How long a rope is required to reach from the top of a building 40 ft. high, to the ground 30 ft. from the base of the building?
9. How many steps 2 ft. 4 in. each will a man take in walking 21.4 miles.

(Extra credit from the editor for knowing what kalsomining is.)

Grammar
1. How many parts of speech are there? Define each.
2. "William struck James." Change the voice of the verb.

Geography
1. Through what waters would a vessel pass in going from England through the Suez Canal to Manila?

Physiology
1. Where is the chief nervous center of the body?

Government
1. Name five county officers, and the principal duties of each.

History
1. Who first discovered the following places: Florida, Pacific Ocean, Mississippi River, St. Lawrence River?
2. During what wars were the following battles fought: Brandywine, Great Meadows, Lundy's Lane, Antietam, Buena Vista.

Yikes! Today we may look back on past education standards as basic or rudimentary, even primitive. I hope you were as astounded as I was at the complexity of this exam. No wonder there were 17-year-olds in the eighth grade.

AFTERWORD

Though this narrative is based on Ivy and Polly's research, as well as other family documents, much was missing from Ivy's original work. I have taken it upon myself to add additional history.

First, immigration records indicate the family did not land at Ellis Island (it didn't exist at the time), but at Castle Garden. The ship Ivy said they travelled on was also incorrect. I took it upon myself to describe what the immigration process was like and imagined what the Harnetts experienced.

From a lecture Tom Harnett delivered, I found the family travelled through New Orleans, a hub for the Southern Pacific railroad. Sadly, I could not find any description of that experience, other than the family finally arrived in a very rainy Los Angeles in October 1889.

I also added stories I found in the press about the family estates in Kent, Ernest (Father) Harnett's involvement with British government, and the Great Depression in British agriculture. Julia (Mother) Harnett's family, living next to Bedlam Hospital for the insane, gave me the opportunity to include a little about that institution. I also discovered her family (the Berrells) involvement in the theater.

In discussing Long Beach schools, I added episodes from local newspapers about Mary Wardlow, Foster Strong, the riot of 1908, a Poly High teacher who tried to evade the WWI draft, and the girls' basketball championship. From a brief newspaper sentence, I found Caroline Harnett had once played on the team.

Additional stories included rainmaking, dry farming, the Bouton well, the Municipal Market, squab, jitney travel, Camp Kearney, the murder of Long Beach butcher Mr. Dames, Empire Day and the Japanese on Signal Hill.

Ivy didn't write much about her brother Jack, but newspaper research allowed me to piece together much of his history, and that both he and Edward found wives in Eureka, California.

Norah left behind a diary about her experiences as a teacher in Ketchikan, Alaska. But I had to piece together Josie's teaching career in Tenakee Village, Sitka District, Alaska, by visiting the museum and historical society in Sitka.

Anne's husband, Frank Kimball, was quite an important man in Wyoming history, and I was able to find much on him in state and local archives.

Ivy ignored writing about her high school years. It wasn't until I searched through Poly High School annuals, that I found she didn't graduate until she was 24, in 1915, the same year as her youngest brother Frank. I surmised she was kept back by her early eye injury. I did feel sad that she felt her biggest accomplishment was her award-winning poem, published at the back of this book. It must have been hard on her seeing the many accomplishments of her sisters, and feeling like she could never live up to them. However, I believe her now published memoirs (which I hope you have enjoyed), will make up for that!

Claudine Burnett
June 2023

ABOUT THE AUTHOR

Ivy Harnett passed away in 1983. She left behind notes on the Harnett's immigration experience, the family farm (the Pacific Squab and Poultry Farm), school days, and what the Long Beach/Signal Hill area was like in the 19th and early 20th centuries. Her niece, Polly Harnett Johnson, compiled the notes but died before a manuscript was written. Historian/author Claudine Burnett promised Polly she would finish the project. Ms. Burnett also found additional material on the family in newspapers, census records, and through correspondence. The result is an enjoyable read which includes family joy, and tragedy, all adding to the fascinating narrative Ivy hoped would someday be published.

INDEX

Floods, 8-9, 43, 44 , 64
Flowers, 10, 22, 37, 46, 47-48, 49-51, 80,
    119, 135
Fourth of July. *See* Holidays:Fourth of
    July
Frazier, Nettie, 18-19, 21
Fruit, 10, 15, 17, 36, 44, 46, 48, 52, 56, 57,
    62, 63-64, 120, 121

G

Gulvin, Ed, 1, 3, 8, 120

H

Hall, Elmer, 26
Halloween. *See* Holidays:Halloween
Hammonton, California, 112-113
Harnett, Alfred, uncle, 1, 69, 93
Harnett, Anna Mary, 122-123
Harnett, Anne, 2, 4-5, 9, 17, 24, 57, 59, 61,
    70, 71, 83, 84, 85, 93, 113-114, 115,
    120, 122, 131, 133, 134, 142
Harnett, Anne Dodd, 93
Harnett, Bessie, 2, 3, 5-7, 16, 17, 18, 26,
    27, 29, 30, 31, 35, 36, 37, 39, 47,
    57, 63, 68-69, 73, 74, 76, 78, 80,
    81, 83-84, 86-87, 91, 92, 96, 97-
    101, 105, 106, 107, 114, 117, 122,
    132, 134
Harnett, Caroline, 2, 4, 6, 11, 16, 28, 61,
    69, 83, 93, 97-98, 106, 134, 141
Harnett, Charlotte, 110, 112, 115, 119
Harnett, Edward, 2, 4-5, 6, 17, 24, 49,
    61, 73, 93, 97, 112, 115-119, 120,
    134, 142
Harnett, Ernest Thomas. *See*
    Harnett, Tom
Harnett, Ernest, father, 1-7, 9, 15, 24, 35,
    41, 42, 44, 45, 46, 51, 56-57, 59, 63,
    64, 65, 66, 67, 69, 71, 80, 83, 93-
    96, 97,117, 120, 134
Harnett, Ethel, 2, 3, 61, 82, 91, 92, 101,
    105-107, 116, 134
Harnett, Frank, 9, 23, 24, 28, 29, 37,
    63, 64, 68-69, 71, 81, 84, 93, 96,

106, 115, 116, 120-123, 131, 134,
    135, 143
Harnett, Frank, uncle, 1, 93, 94, 120
Harnett, Geoffrey, 2, 3, 93, 96-97, 134
Harnett, Helen, 2, 4, 5, 11, 20, 59-60,
    69, 72-73, 76, 85, 93, 104, 120,
    133, 134
Harnett, Ivy, ix-x, xii, 38-39, 72-75, 106,
    110-111, 131, 137, 141-142
Harnett, Jack, 2, 3, 65, 82, 91, 92, 105-106,
    111-113, 115, 134, 142
Harnett, Jane. *See* Harnett, Bessie
Harnett, John. *See* Harnett, Jack
Harnett, Josie, 2, 4, 5, 17, 20-21, 22, 23,
    24, 59-60, 69, 71, 74, 85, 93, 96,
    97, 98, 107, 109-110, 115, 117, 120,
    122, 131, 132, 133, 142
Harnett, Julia Berrell, mother, 2-6, 17, 39,
    43, 44, 49, 61-62, 64, 69, 70, 71,
    73, 77, 81, 82, 83, 84, 89-92, 94-95,
    96, 97, 105, 106, 110, 115, 117, 120,
    121, 134
Harnett, Kathleen, 23, 27, 28, 29, 49, 68-
    69, 72, 76-77, 84, 90, 93, 94, 100,
    106, 119, 131-134, 135
Harnett, Leonora, 111, 112
Harnett, Norah, 2, 4, 5, 7, 20-21, 22, 23,
    24, 59, 69, 76, 85, 93, 107-109, 110,
    117, 120, 131, 132, 133, 142
Harnett, Thomas, grandfather, 1
Harnett, Tom, 2, 3, 5-7, 9, 59, 62, 64, 68,
    75-76, 77, 78, 84, 85, 87, 92, 94,
    96, 101-104, 111, 115, 116-117, 123,
    131, 133, 134, 135, 141
Holidays
    Christmas, 8, 82-85
    Empire Day, 86-87
    Fourth of July, 71, 80-81
Halloween, 81
    Washington's birthday, 20-21
Horses, 15, 16, 20, 37, 38, 39, 41, 46, 56,
    58, 59-61, 73-74, 77, 78, 92, 93,
    118, 121, 123
Hospitals
    Bedlam, 89-90, 141
    Memorial, 101

146

Printed in the United States
by Baker & Taylor Publisher Services